# HALLOWED GROUND

*Battlefields of the Civil War*

# HALLOWED

# GROUND
## Battlefields of the Civil War

PHOTOGRAPHS BY ALAN BRIERE

TEXT BY HARRISON HUNT

**MALLARD PRESS**

**An Imprint of BDD Promotional Book Company, Inc.**
666 Fifth Avenue, New York, N.Y. 10103

 An M & M Book

(Previous pages) *The silent sentry of Gettysburg. General Hancock's statue on Cemetery Ridge in winter.*

(These pages) *The statue atop the 137th Pennsylvania Monument at Antietam set against a brooding Maryland sky.*

(Following pages) *A bust of Abraham Lincoln at Gettysburg National Military Park, site of the president's famed address.*

An Imprint of BDD Promotional Book Company, Inc.
666 Fifth Avenue
New York, NY 10103

Copyright © 1990 by Moore & Moore Publishing

First published in the United States of America in 1990 by The Mallard Press.

ISBN 0 7924 5213-5

## An M & M Book

*Hallowed Ground* was prepared and produced by Moore & Moore Publishing, 11 W. 19th Street, New York, NY 10011.

*Project Director & Editor* Gary Fishgall

*Senior Editorial Assistant* Shirley Vierheller; *Editorial Assistants* Lisa Pike, Ben McLaughlin, David Blankenship; *Research, Historic Photos* Lucinda Stellini, Maxine Dormer; *Copy Editor* Bert N. Zelman of Publishers Workshop Inc.

*Designer* Binns & Lubin/Martin Lubin

*Separations and Printing* Regent Publishing Services Ltd., Hong Kong

*Typesetting* Sharon Brant Typography

# CONTENTS

*But, in a larger sense, we cannot dedicate—*
*we cannot consecrate—we cannot hallow this*
*ground. The brave men, living and dead, who*
*struggled here have consecrated it far above*
*our poor power to add or detract.*

*Abraham Lincoln*

Address at Gettysburg
November 19, 1863

# INTRODUCTION

No event in U.S. history has captured the imagination of the American people like the Civil War. Indeed, the sheer magnitude of the struggle is awesome: three million young men—half the country's male population between the ages of 15 and 40—joined the armed forces of the North and South to fight for the causes they believed in; of these men, more than 600,000 (over 20 percent) never returned, a higher number of fatalities than in all other U.S. wars through Korea *combined*. The continuing interest in the Civil War is also due to the primary issues over which its bloody battles were fought—states' rights and the status of Americans of African descent—issues which are still with us.

Adding to the fascination with this epic struggle are the dozens of battle sites that have been preserved as some of the best-marked battlefields in the world. The National Park Service alone administers 21 Civil War battle sites containing more than 50,000 acres in 11 states. Additional battlegrounds such as Saylor's Creek and New Market have been preserved by interested state governments and private organizations. By visiting these hallowed grounds—the farmlands and forests where soldiers in blue and gray struggled and died—people from all over the world can gain a unique perspective on the war. Only by *traversing* these sites can a person get the full sense of the terrain where the fighting occurred. Only by *seeing* the battlefields can one truly appreciate the immensity of what took place there long ago.

Alan Briere's photographs have beautifully captured the spirit of 17 of these battlefields for the readers of *Hallowed Ground*. His unique vision, as seen in these splendid color photos, is evocative and moving.

Briere's contemporary photo studies also include images taken at the 1989 re-creations of the battles of New Market, Virginia, and Monocacy, Maryland (which occurred in May 1864 and July 1864, respectively). These photographs appear throughout the book to provide readers with additional insight into the conflict, as do images from the Civil War period that show the principal generals on each side and the fields of battle as they appeared in the 1860s.

The text gives the reader a clear overview of what led up to and happened at each of the 17 battle sites. Obviously, reducing campaigns such as Gettysburg and Vicksburg to short essays precludes much extensive detail, but the historic narratives provide a basic understanding of how the battles were fought and enhance an appreciation for the photos.

Whether you are a Civil War aficionado or a casual reader, a regular visitor to these renowned battlefields or someone who has never seen them before, *Hallowed Ground* will transport you to all of the important places where the war was fought—from Fort Sumter to Appomattox. It is a journey worth the taking, for its path retraces one of the most heroic and tragic episodes in human history—the American Civil War.

(Opposite) *Sunset viewed through the hilt of General Warren's sword in this detail of the Little Round Top Statue at Gettysburg National Military Park.*

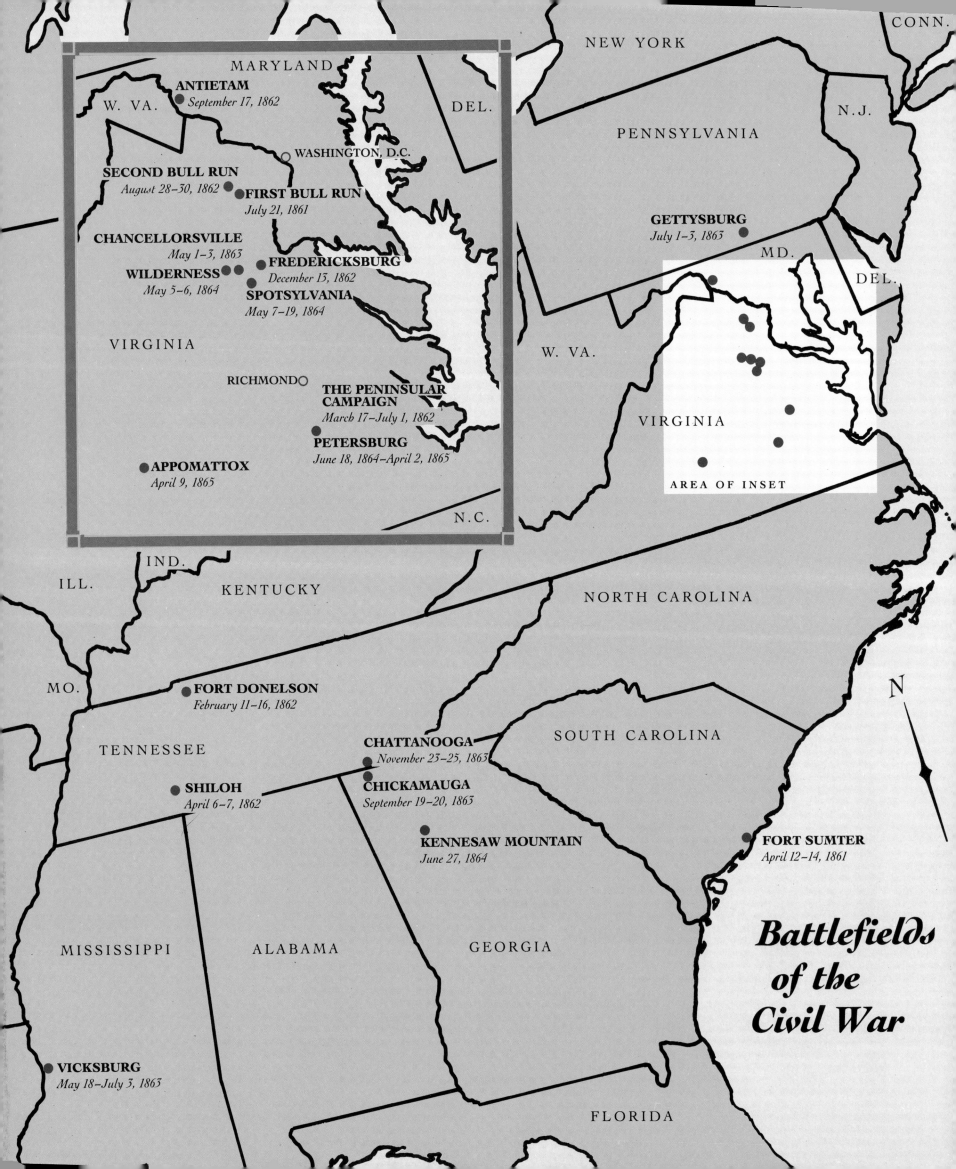

**MARYLAND**

**ANTIETAM**
*September 17, 1862*

W. VA.

DEL.

WASHINGTON, D.C.

**SECOND BULL RUN**
*August 28–30, 1862*

**FIRST BULL RUN**
*July 21, 1861*

**CHANCELLORSVILLE**
*May 1–3, 1863*

**FREDERICKSBURG**
*December 13, 1862*

**WILDERNESS**
*May 5–6, 1864*

**SPOTSYLVANIA**
*May 7–19, 1864*

VIRGINIA

RICHMOND

**THE PENINSULAR
CAMPAIGN**
*March 17–July 1, 1862*

**PETERSBURG**
*June 18, 1864–April 2, 1865*

**APPOMATTOX**
*April 9, 1865*

N.C.

CONN.

NEW YORK

PENNSYLVANIA

N.J.

**GETTYSBURG**
*July 1–3, 1863*

MD.

DEL.

W. VA.

VIRGINIA

**AREA OF INSET**

ILL.

IND.

MO.

KENTUCKY

TENNESSEE

**FORT DONELSON**
*February 11–16, 1862*

**SHILOH**
*April 6–7, 1862*

**CHATTANOOGA**
*November 23–25, 1863*

**CHICKAMAUGA**
*September 19–20, 1863*

NORTH CAROLINA

SOUTH CAROLINA

**KENNESAW MOUNTAIN**
*June 27, 1864*

**FORT SUMTER**
*April 12–14, 1861*

N

MISSISSIPPI

ALABAMA

GEORGIA

*Battlefields
of the
Civil War*

**VICKSBURG**
*May 18–July 3, 1863*

FLORIDA

# FORT SUMTER

The Civil War—the four years of fighting which broke apart and then reunited a country, claiming the lives of more than 620,000 Americans in the process—began with the shots fired at Fort Sumter. But the shells which exploded over Charleston harbor in April 1861 were merely the sparks igniting a long-simmering struggle over slavery versus freedom, and states' rights versus national unity, that had gradually been dividing North and South for decades. The situation finally came to the breaking point in November 1860 with the election of the first Republican President of the United States, Abraham Lincoln. Although the Republicans did not oppose slavery in states where it existed, the party platform called for banning it in U.S. territories—and, therefore, the new states that would eventually be created from those territories. This meant that the institution of slavery would be forever limited to 15 states and that the carefully preserved legislative balance between slaveholding and free states in the U.S. Senate would be inexorably tipped against slavery, sooner or later spelling the end for the South's "peculiar institution."

Consequently, the slave states of the South saw Lincoln's election as a direct threat to their way of life, a threat which could not go unanswered. The first state to respond was South Carolina, a hotbed of states' rights agitation that had first considered secession from the Union 30 years earlier during Andrew Jackson's administration. Within days of Lincoln's victory, the South Carolina militia began stockpiling arms. On December 3, 1860, a

*In 1861, Maj. Robert Anderson's small band of Union soldiers returned the Confederates' fire from the protection of these masonry casemates within Sumter's walls.*

*(Previous page) Fort Sumter displays the flags that flew over the partially completed fortress during the Civil War. From left to right, they are Carolina's Palmetto flag, the Stars and Bars (the Confederate first national flag), and the Stars and Stripes.*

The brickwork in this passageway at Fort Moultrie, which Major Anderson abandoned in favor of Fort Sumter on December 26, 1860, is typical of the massive construction of Charleston's defenses. Advances in artillery technology made such masonry fortifications obsolete by the end of the Civil War.

(Opposite) The Powder Magazine at Fort Moultrie. Many of the 4000 rounds fired at Sumter on April 12 and 13, 1861, came from this building.

Congress of Secession convened, and on December 20 South Carolina formally seceded from the Union.

As these political events were transpiring, attention began focusing on the most visible symbols of the Federal government in South Carolina, the U.S. Army fortifications in Charleston. These included an arsenal in the city and several forts designed to protect Charleston harbor from foreign warships: Fort Moultrie, headquarters to the city's small Federal garrison, at the eastern entrance to the harbor; Castle Pinckney, on an island near the mainland, and Fort Johnson, near the western entrance to the harbor, both unmanned and essentially abandoned; and the unfinished Fort Sumter, which lay under construction on a small island midway between

Forts Moultrie and Johnson. The new South Carolina government wanted the Federal troops to leave Charleston and turn these fortifications over to them; the lame-duck administration of President James Buchanan, marking time until Lincoln's inauguration, was paralyzed by indecision and did not know how to respond to South Carolina's demands.

In the middle of all this turmoil was the commander of the 74 U.S. Army officers and enlisted men in Charleston, Maj. Robert Anderson. A Southerner by birth but loyal to the Union, Anderson had only been appointed to this command on November 15, replacing a Yankee officer the Carolinians found offensive. Anderson immediately realized that his limited forces could not possibly defend Fort Moultrie,

*Fort Sumter shortly after Major Anderson's surrender, showing some of the damage caused by the Confederate bombardment. The fort was further damaged when it was recaptured by the Union in 1865. (South Caroliniana Library, University of South Carolina, Columbia, SC)*

which was designed to deal with attacks from the sea, not the land. He knew that the island-based Fort Sumter, with its 5-foot-thick brick walls towering 40 feet above the deep waters of Charleston harbor, was a much better defensive position, but he had no authorization to move his men there. South Carolina officials, also recognizing Sumter's strategic importance, notified Washington that they did not want the fort manned,

and they assigned a boat to patrol the channel between Moultrie and Sumter to prevent any transfer of U.S. troops.

After South Carolina's secession on December 20, Major Anderson finally received permission from Washington to move his men to Fort Sumter if attacked, or if attack seemed imminent— and there was no question in his mind about that. On December 26, 1860, he secretly had the garrison's dependents moved to Fort Johnson, disabled the cannon at Fort Moultrie, and after dark had his men row out to Sumter, narrowly avoiding detection.

While Major Anderson and his men prepared Sumter for a siege and the South Carolina militia busied itself installing new batteries of artillery around Charleston harbor, other Southern states were following South Carolina's lead and leaving the Union. By February 8, 1861, seven states had seceded and agreed to form a confederation which would represent their common interests and deal with the U.S. military installations, including forts and arsenals, within their boundaries. On March 3, the newly elected President of the Confederate States of America, Jefferson Davis, dispatched Lt. Gen. Pierre G. T. Beauregard of Louisiana to take charge of Charleston's defenses, and the South Carolina militia no longer stood alone against the U.S. Army.

Meanwhile, the United States itself was finally preparing to act decisively on the matter of Fort Sumter. While an unarmed relief ship, *Star of the West,* had been sent to Major Anderson's aid in early January, it was driven away by the Charleston artillery and no attempt at reinforcing the fort had been made since. By the time

*Sumter's uppermost gun level—the barbette—which was filled in with earth after the war. The field artillery pictured here is actually much smaller than the fort's original armaments.*

*Maj. Robert Anderson, commander of the Federal garrison at Sumter. After the North recaptured the fort in 1865, Anderson—then a major general—returned to raise the U.S. flag he had lowered at Sumter's surrender four years earlier. (Library of Congress)*

(Above right) *This monument on the fort's parade ground pays tribute to the small Union garrison which defended Sumter during the Confederate bombardment. To the rear are some of the fort's artillery casemates.*

of Abraham Lincoln's inauguration as 16th President of the United States on March 4, 1861 (inaugurations were held in March until 1937), the new Chief Executive was committed to maintaining a firm stance against secession. He chose to make that stand at Fort Sumter but had to move quickly as Anderson's supplies were dwindling and Sumter would be starved into surrender if it received no aid by April.

President Lincoln ordered a supply ship and naval escort to Charleston on April 8, notifying Governor Francis W. Pickens of South Carolina that he would not attack the port or attempt to reinforce Sumter unless his unarmed supply ship was fired upon first—thereby placing the responsibility for starting war on the Southerners. The Confederates did not wait for Lincoln's ships to arrive. On April 10, General Beauregard was ordered to demand Sumter's surrender and, if it

was not given, to shell the fort into submission. Major Anderson refused Beauregard's demand, and the Confederate bombardment began at 4:30 on the morning of April 12, 1861. Anderson returned the fire as best he could, but only 60 of the fort's 135 guns were in place and he had only a fraction of the 650 troops needed to man Sumter's works. After enduring 34 hours of shelling in which some 4000 rounds were fired, Major Anderson surrendered; his garrison withdrew from Fort Sumter at noon of April 14. The following day, President Lincoln declared that a state of war existed between the United States and its rebellious territories and called for 75,000 volunteer troops. By May 20 a total of 11 states had joined the Confederacy and the bloodiest war in American history was under way.

GENERAL
BARNARD ELLIOTT BEE,
OF SOUTH CAROLINA,
COMMANDER, THIRD BRIGADE,
ARMY OF THE SHENANDOAH,
WAS KILLED HERE JULY 21, 1861.

JUST BEFORE HIS DEATH,
TO RALLY HIS SCATTERED TROOPS,
HE GAVE THE COMMAND:
"FORM, FORM, THERE STANDS JACKSON
LIKE A STONE WALL,
RALLY BEHIND THE VIRGINIANS"

PRESENTED BY
MARY TALIAFERRO THOMPSON
SOUTHERN MEMORIAL ASS'N.
OF WASHINGTON, D. C. - JULY 21, 1936

FIRST BULL RUN

*Stone Bridge, scene of the Union army's early-morning feint against the Confederates at Manassas. Later in the day it was clogged with retreating Yankees.*

(Previous page) *This memorial honors Confederate Brig. Gen. Bernard E. Bee on Henry House Hill. Bee, who gave "Stonewall" Jackson his nickname, was killed in action here.*

Following the fall of Fort Sumter, most Northerners demanded swift action against the South. Patriotic rallies echoed with cries of "On to Richmond!"—the Confederate capital—and volunteers signed up for 90 days' service, ample time, they believed, for the war to be fought and won.

Although U.S. troops began concentrating around Washington, D.C., in April and May 1861, no major move against the Confederacy had been attempted by the beginning of July. Concerned that the enlistments of many 90-day volunteers would soon be up, the U.S. Congress met in an extraordinary session on July 4, urging military action.

Although the commander of the Union Army, Brig. Gen. Irvin McDowell, realized that his troops needed extensive training before they would be ready for battle, he gave in to political pressures to fight quickly. His target was the Confederate forces gathered 25 miles away from Washington, D.C., at Manassas, Virginia.

Manassas was a small rural village at the junction of two strategically important railroad lines, the Orange & Alexandria Railroad, which ran southwest from Alexandria into central Virginia, and the Manassas Gap Railroad, which ran westward into the Shenandoah Valley. Confederate troops under the command of Lt. Gen. Pierre G. T. Beauregard of Sumter fame had been at Manassas since early May. By July, 22,000 men were massed there along an 8-mile stretch of the Bull Run creek, which meandered southeasterly through the countryside north of the railroads.

Union General McDowell began moving his 35,000 troops from the Washington area southwest toward Manassas on July 16. His raw recruits marched slowly in the summer heat, and on July 18 were still 4 miles from Bull Run, in Centreville, Virginia. Here, McDowell took two more days to scout the territory and plan his attack. These delays not only eliminated much of McDowell's element of surprise but also allowed Beauregard to be reinforced. On July 20, a force of

*A monument to the Union's 14th Brooklyn Militia Regiment. Attired in distinctive red and blue uniforms, the hard-fighting unit gained the sobriquet ''red-legged devils from Brooklyn'' at First Bull Run.*

*The clashing armies swirled past the Robinson House, pictured here, as they worked their way south to Henry House Hill.*

Henry House Hill is named for the home of
Judith Carter Henry located there. The house
(seen in the background at right) was destroyed
at the Second Battle of Bull Run but has been
reconstructed.

The 84-year-old Mrs. Henry refused to leave
her home during the fighting. Late in the
afternoon a cannonball smashed through her
bedroom window (above), killing her. The
battle's only civilian casualty, she is buried
nearby.

8300 men under Gen. Joseph E. Johnston arrived from near Winchester, Virginia, via the Manassas Gap Railroad—the first major troop movement by rail in history—and 1200 more men marched in from the south, giving the Confederates a total of 33,000 troops.

McDowell moved ahead with his plans for battle unaware that Beauregard's forces were now equal to his. The Union commander decided to concentrate his attack on the section of the Confederate line furthest from Centreville, at Sudley Ford, one of several crossing points along Bull Run. His strategy called for marching most of his troops northwest to Sudley Ford by a circuitous route screened from Confederate eyes and sweeping down on Beauregard's left. Other U.S.

units sent to Stone Bridge opposite the center of the Confederate line would provide diversionary fire before the main thrust at Sudley. Additional troops were detailed to protect the Blackburn's Ford crossing on the eastern end of the Confederate line. While this action was necessary to prevent nearby rebel forces from counterattacking the Union's main body, it drew off McDowell's reserves in the process.

McDowell finally put his plan into action on July 21, 1861, and immediately ran into trouble. The march, which was supposed to have brought his troops to Sudley around sunrise, did not begin until 4:30 a.m. The 8-mile route took much longer to cover than McDowell had estimated, and Union soldiers under Brig. Gen.

David Hunter and Brig. Gen. S. P. Heintzelman did not reach Sudley until close to 9 o'clock that morning. The U.S. troops assigned to attack Stone Bridge, only 4 miles from Centreville, arrived much earlier and started their diversionary actions hours before Hunter's troops were in place (the bridge was rebuilt after the battle and is now a major site at the battlefield park). By 8:30 a.m. the Confederate commander at Stone Bridge, Col. Nathan G. Evans, suspected that the Union fighting opposite his posi-

(Opposite) *One of the Confederate artillery batteries on Henry House Hill that drove the Federal troops from Bull Run.*

*The railroad at Manassas Junction, shown here in 1862. The First Battle of Bull Run saw history's first major troop movement by rail. (Library of Congress)*

The scene at Henry House Hill was similar to that seen here at the re-created Battle of New Market, Virginia. Civil War troops used black powder in their rifles and cannon that gave off heavy smoke, often obscuring the line of fire.

*Lt. Gen. Pierre Gustave Toutant Beauregard, conqueror of Fort Sumter and commander of the victorious Confederate forces at First Bull Run. (Library of Congress)*

(Opposite) *Gen. Thomas J. ("Stonewall") Jackson, immortalized in stone, still stands guard over Bull Run near the battlefield's visitors' center.*

*Maj. Gen. Irvin McDowell, who was unlucky enough to command the Union army at its first defeat. (Library of Congress)*

tion was merely a feint. Spotting the Union column moving toward Sudley Ford, Evans realized that the main attack was aimed at his left and quickly moved to face it.

Evans placed his regiments perpendicular to Bull Run Creek at a stone house (still a major landmark on the battlefield) and nearby Matthews Hill, facing north toward Sudley Ford. Here, the battle began in earnest when Federal forces crossed Bull Run at about 9:15 a.m. The Yankees pressed the attack, and by 12 noon the Confederates were falling back in retreat toward Henry House, a small home (reconstructed since the battle) set on a plateau south of Matthews Hill. At this point, Confederate Gen. Bernard E. Bee, attempting to halt his retreating forces, pointed to an impassive Virginia general standing motionless with his troops and shouted, "Look! There stands Jackson like a stone wall! Rally behind the Virginians!" Thus Thomas J. ("Stonewall") Jackson, one of the South's greatest generals, earned his nickname.

The Confederates did rally around Jackson's position on Henry House Hill. Then, during a lull in the fighting between 1 and 2 o'clock, they were reinforced by 1700 badly needed troops who had just arrived by railroad from the Shenandoah Valley. When the battle resumed around 2 o'clock, both sides fought valiantly against fatigue and the blistering summer heat, as well as each other. Federal troops overran Henry House Hill five times that afternoon and were driven back each time. At 4 o'clock, the Yankees grouped for a final assault, but the Confederates—further strengthened by fresh troops from the eastern end of the Confederate line—swept down the slopes of Henry House Hill and drove the Yankees from the field. Exhausted and dispirited, the Federal soldiers scattered toward Washington in a rout, their line of retreat clogged by ambulances and supply wagons. Also in retreat were sightseeing Congressmen and other U.S. government officials who had driven to the battlefield from Washington expecting to see the winning of the war while they munched on picnic lunches. The Confederates—said to be as disorganized in victory as their foes were in defeat—were in no shape to pursue the Union forces, which made their way back to Washington over the next few days.

The fierce fighting and more than 3500 casualties at the First Battle of Bull Run (or First Manassas, as the Confederates called it) jolted both North and South. No longer would there be naive talk of ending the war in 90 days, and never again would the public look upon the bloody struggle between these armies as outdoor entertainment. Nor would Northern generals send untrained troops into battle. While the North prepared itself for a long, hard war, the South had an opportunity to solidify its position in the east.

*The inscription of the Civil War's first battlefield monument, erected at Henry House Hill in 1865.*

# FORT DONELSON

*The inside of a cabin used as winter quarters by Donelson's garrison, with another seen through the doorway. These structures were small and drafty, but they still provided better shelter than the canvas tents used during the rest of the year.*

(Previous page) *The Confederate Monument was erected in 1933 by the United Daughters of the Confederacy in memory of the Southern soldiers who defended Fort Donelson.*

In the western theatre—that is, in the states bordering the Mississippi River valley—the war started badly for the Union as badly as it had in the east. Within a month of the First Battle of Bull Run, in August 1861, Union forces in Missouri were defeated in their first battle, at Wilson's Creek. This Confederate success was followed by others and, by November 1861, the need for a face-saving Federal victory was becoming acute.

The Lincoln administration addressed this problem by replacing the luckless Union commander in Missouri, John C. Frémont, with Maj. Gen. Henry W. Halleck, a talented administrator who later became Lincoln's chief military adviser. Halleck and Brig. Gen. Don Carlos Buell, who commanded the U.S. forces in central Kentucky, were assigned to drive Gen. Albert S. Johnston's Confederate troops from western Kentucky and Tennessee.

Halleck's forces were headquartered in southern Illinois at the junction of the Mississippi and Ohio Rivers. A few miles to the east, the Tennessee and Cumberland Rivers flowed into the waters of the Ohio from deep inside Tennessee. If Halleck's Yankees could secure these waterways, they could attack Johnston's army on its home ground at will. To prevent this, the Confederates established two riverside forts near the Kentucky–Tennessee border: Fort Henry, on the Tennessee River, and Fort Donelson, overlooking the Cumberland.

In January 1862, Halleck began exploring ways to capture these Confederate positions. One of his officers, a little-known brigadier general named Ulysses Simpson Grant, came up with an ingenious plan for seizing Fort Henry: he would take 15,000 men up the Ohio on riverboats, land to the north of the fort, and attack it from the inland side, while U.S. Navy gunboats shelled it from the Tennessee River. Halleck approved the plan, and Grant, supported by Navy Flag Officer (later Read Adm.) Andrew H. Foote, arrived near Fort Henry on February 5. Foote's armor-plated gun-

*Brig. Gen. Ulysses Simpson Grant, "the Hero of Fort Donelson," in full-dress uniform. Shortly after this photo was taken he trimmed his beard to its now more familiar appearance. (Library of Congress)*

*Brig. Gen. Simon Bolivar Buckner, the Confederate officer who took over the command of Fort Donelson after his two superiors slipped away. (Library of Congress)*

*From batteries like this one, Confederate artillerymen held back the Union gunboats on the Cumberland River (seen in the background), forcing Grant to lay siege to Donelson from the landward side.*

While the cabins at Fort Donelson served as the garrison's winter quarters, the soldiers of the North and South lived in tents for most of the year. Several common styles are shown here. From the left (behind the coffee pot) are an officer's wall tent; an "A," or wedge, tent, which slept four; and an overhead "fly." A row of wedge tents is seen below.

(Right and below right) *Details of the Confederate Monument, dedicated to the 13,000 men who held Donelson to the end.*

boats, in use for the first time, proved so powerful against Fort Henry's limited defenses that before Grant's troops even had time to surround the fort, Henry's commander ordered 2500 of his men to retreat to Fort Donelson and surrendered his near-empty stronghold to the Navy on February 6.

Encouraged by this success, Grant decided to capture Fort Donelson as well. While some of Foote's gunboats steamed upstream to secure the Tennessee River from the north, Grant prepared for the 12-mile march east to Donelson. On February 11, he and Foote were on their way.

When Grant arrived at Donelson a day later, he discovered the fort to be better armed and better fortified than Fort Henry had been, with two batteries of artillery overlooking the Cumberland River. The fort itself consisted of a 15-acre stockade surrounded by some 3 miles of trenches. These works were manned by more than 16,000 Confederates, including 12,000 men rushed to the scene from Bowling Green, Kentucky, by Confederate General Johnston. Fearing the entrapment of his entire army with Grant to his west and Buell moving toward him from the north, Johnston needed these forces at Donelson to forestall Grant so that he and the rest of his army could safely retreat to Nashville where it could recoup to fight another day.

Finding his 15,000 men unexpectedly outnumbered at Donelson, Grant sent for reinforcements. Ten thousand additional troops arrived on February 13 and encircled the Confederate trenches. When the Navy gunboats arrived the following day, hope for a repeat of the Fort Henry victory swept the Union camp, but this was not to be. The gunboats, which approached too close to fire effectively, could not destroy Donelson's defenses and were themselves badly battered by the fort's artillery. Despite such damage, however, the gunboats still commanded the river at the end of the day, and between them and Grant's troops the

HONOR THEIR VALOR, EMULATE THE DEVOTION WITH WHICH THEY GAVE THEMSELVES TO THE SERVICE OF THEIR COUNTRY, LET IT NEVER BE SAID THAT THEIR SONS IN THESE SOUTHERN STATES HAVE FORGOTTEN THEIR NOBLE EXAMPLE.

Confederate forces in Fort Donelson were trapped.

Assessing their situation, the Confederate commanders decided that they had to attempt to break through the Union lines and link up with the rest of General Johnston's forces around Nashville. On the morning of February 15, they attacked the right end of Grant's line south of the village of Dover. Taking the Yankees by surprise, the Confederates pushed through at Forge Road—today part of the Fort Donelson National Battlefield—but their commander, Gen. John B. Floyd, suddenly fearful of a Union counterattack, ordered his men back to their original positions in the trenches. Shortly thereafter Grant, who had been away conferring with Flag Officer Foote, returned to the scene of battle and placed his troops on the offensive, driving back the Confederate lines closest to the stockade and tightening his grip on Donelson. That night General Floyd, seeing the hopelessness of his situation, escaped with about 2000 men, leaving Brig. Gen. Simon Bolivar Buckner to face the Union besiegers.

*The Dover Hotel, where Brig. Gen. Simon B. Buckner unconditionally surrendered to Brig. Gen. Ulysses S. Grant on February 16, 1862.*

*A close-up of the Dover Hotel. It is one of only two extant buildings to see major surrenders during the Civil War. Even McLean House, where Lee surrendered to Grant in 1865, is a modern reconstruction.*

The next morning, Buckner asked the Northern commander for terms and Grant issued his now-famous reply that "No terms except an unconditional and immediate surrender can be accepted." On February 16, 1862, Buckner complied, surrendering his 13,000-man garrison at the Dover Hotel, which still stands as a museum adjacent to the battlefield.

The campaign for Forts Henry and Donelson had successfully driven Johnston's Confederates from Kentucky and opened Tennessee to the Union army. More importantly, it gave the Union its first major victory and created a new national hero—Gen. U. S. ("Unconditional Surrender") Grant.

SHILOH

*Cannon at the Peach Orchard, where the gunfire amid the trees was so heavy that the blossoms fell like snow.*

*This crude cabin adjacent to Shiloh's Peach Orchard was a battlefield landmark for both Northern and Southern soldiers. It was occupied by a tenant farmer named Manse George during the fighting.*

*(Previous page) Gen. Albert S. Johnston's Confederates first attacked the unsuspecting Union forces here at Fraley Field at dawn on April 6, 1862.*

With the fall of Fort Donelson, Gen. Albert S. Johnston's 20,000 troops could no longer hold Nashville, Tennessee, for the Confederacy. General Grant controlled the Cumberland River, which led directly from Fort Donelson to Nashville, and he could send 40,000 men there at will. If that were not bad enough for Johnston, 35,000 Union troops under Brig. Gen. Don Carlos Buell were heading toward Nashville from Kentucky. Faced with these overwhelming odds, the Confederate commander had no choice but to abandon Nashville. Accordingly, he marched his army out of the city on February 23, 1862, just one day before Buell's Yankees arrived. This was a serious blow to the South. Nashville was one of the few major manufacturing centers in the largely agrarian Confederacy, and its loss would be sorely felt in the years ahead.

Johnston's forces headed southwest across the Mississippi border to Corinth, a vital railroad link between the eastern and western Confederacy. Arriving in early March 1862, they were soon reinforced by fresh troops that swelled their ranks to more than 42,000 men. This army was thoroughly reorganized by Johnston and Lt. Gen. Pierre G. T. Beauregard, who had just been assigned as his second-in-command, and the new recruits were put to drilling for combat.

The Union Army gave the Confederate troops in Corinth plenty of time to practice their manual of arms. Although Grant had wanted to pursue Johnston immediately, his superior, Maj. Gen. Henry W. Halleck, insisted on a more cautious approach: Grant was to sail down the Tennessee River to a spot just north of the Mississippi border and wait there for General Buell's forces to join him before embarking on a campaign against the enemy. It was close to the end of March before Grant's troops reached their rendezvous point—Pittsburg Landing, Tennessee—a riverboat stopping place near an isolated country chapel called Shiloh Church. This delay gave Johnston's Confederates more than enough time to regroup and plan their next move.

*Gen. Albert S. Johnston, the daring Confederate commander who was killed at Shiloh. (Library of Congress)*

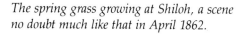

*The spring grass growing at Shiloh, a scene no doubt much like that in April 1862.*

The move Johnston decided on was a bold one. He knew that his 42,000 men could not take a stand against the 75,000 troops that Grant and Buell would have once they joined forces, so he decided to attack Grant before Buell arrived. The Southerners' only chance lay in dealing Grant's Yankees a stunning blow that would send them back north shattered and in retreat.

Johnston's troops moved out of Corinth on April 3, 1862. They were supposed to arrive near Shiloh the next day, but the rebels—mostly new recruits on their first long march—moved slowly and did not finish their 18-mile trek until late on April 5. General Beauregard felt that the attack had lost the crucial element of surprise and that the troops were unprepared for combat (in short, it was looking like a Confederate version of the Union attack on Bull Run the year before). He therefore urged Johnston to return to Corinth. But the Confederate commander refused to consider a change of plans and ordered an attack on Grant's position at dawn on April 6.

Luck was with Johnston. Grant's troops were scattered along a 3-mile line of high ground running north and south of the Shiloh Church about 2 miles inland from Pittsburg Landing. Convinced that the Confederates would not dare attack him, Grant had neither fortified the Yankee lines nor sent patrols into the countryside. As a result, Johnston's dawn attack was an

(Opposite) *Retreating Federal troops rallied behind the safety of these artillery pieces at "Grant's Last Line," in the northeast corner of the battlefield.*

(Above and left) *Details of the Confederate Monument, which honors the 10,000 Southern soldiers who fell at "Bloody Shiloh."*

(Far left) *One of the five Confederate burial trenches at Shiloh. More than 700 Southern soldiers lie in this mass grave, their names known only to God.*

almost complete surprise, undetected by Union sentries until the lead Confederate units were practically on top of them.

The rebels swept into the Federal camps from the southwest, firing the first shots of the Battle of Shiloh at Fraley Field, today a major stop on the battlefield tour. Wave after wave of men were soon pushing the entire Federal line to the northeast, back toward Pittsburg Landing. The fighting was unlike anything yet seen in the war. The Federal units, caught off guard and isolated from each other, were left to defend themselves as best they could without hope of reinforcement. Some broke ranks and ran all the way back to the Tennessee River, cowering behind the bluffs near Pittsburg Landing. Others, such as those serving under Brig. Gen. William Tecumseh Sherman, stood their ground as long as they could against the rebel onslaught, pulling back only when threatened with being enveloped.

The Union's problems that morning were complicated by the fact that General Grant was off the field at the time of the Confederate attack—just as at Donelson. He was 7 miles to the north awaiting Buell and so was unable to coordinate the defense. When he returned to Pittsburg Landing around noon, he immediately took to the field, where he found troops under the command of Brig. Gen. Benjamin M. Prentiss making a stand at a low road—Shiloh's famous "Sunken Road"—near the crest of a small hill at the center of the battlefield. Grant ordered Prentiss to hold that position at all costs while he organized a defensive line at the landing. Prentiss and his men complied valiantly, holding off 11 Confederate assaults during the afternoon. Indeed, the firing on both sides was so intense that the site would thereafter be known as the "Hornets' Nest." The position was not overrun (and Prentiss captured) until it was pounded by

*In the beauty of early spring it is difficult to imagine the fierce fighting which earned this spot the name ''Hornets' Nest.''*

The Confederate infantry soldier's basic fighting equipment is shown at left hanging on a tentpole. The rifle is a .57 caliber muzzle-loading Enfield, one of the two most common rifles used in the war. The bayonet hanging next to it was designed to be used as a spearpoint on the end of the rifle; in fact, bayonets were seldom drawn in combat, but often used to toast bread over campfires. The square-shaped pouch was the soldier's cartridge box, which held his ammunition. Similar Union equipment may be seen above in the detail from a Shiloh monument. Clockwise from left are a cartridge box, a rifle (section), a cap pouch, a bayonet and scabbard, a canteen, and a belt with a "U.S." buckle.

a battery of 62 artillery pieces brought up by Confederate Gen. Daniel Ruggles around 5 p.m., and by that time Grant had been able to establish his fallback position near the river.

While the Yankees and Confederates were battling for the Hornets' Nest, Confederate General Johnston circled around to the southeast to check another scene of intense fighting in a peach orchard. Here the gunfire was so heavy that the peach blossoms shot from the trees were said to have

fallen like snow. One of the bullets fired there caught Johnston in the leg and, before medical help could reach him, he bled to death, at a spot now marked by a monument on the battlefield. With his death the South lost one of its finest officers, and the Confederate army at Shiloh lost its driving force.

By the time the fighting at Shiloh wound down at dusk, the Confederates held most of the field, but they had lost almost 10,000 men. Although they had inflicted an equal number of casualties on the Union side, they had

failed to destroy Grant's army in one clean sweep (which they had needed to do in order to win). Grant—aided by Prentiss's holding action at the Hornets' Nest—had been able to reorganize his shattered troops on a defensive line running west from the landing and was already planning for the next day's fighting. That night, the first of Buell's men arrived to reinforce Grant. The fresh troops—20,000 strong—were more than enough to make up for the day's casualties. Thus the Confederates lost whatever advantage they had gained that day.

The next morning Grant placed his troops on the offensive, driving the Confederates back toward Shiloh Church. The Southerners tried to stem the Union advance at Water Oaks Pond, a little to the north of the church, but General Beauregard—who took command of the Southern army after Johnston's death—saw that they could not win against Grant's superior numbers and ordered a retreat to Corinth. The two days of fighting at "Bloody Shiloh" had cost both armies a total of 23,000 men and lost western Tennessee for the Confederacy.

*This cannon is situated at the Sunken Road between the Hornets' Nest and the Peach Orchard, scene of some of Shiloh's harshest fighting.*

*The monument of the 77th Pennsylvania Regiment.*

PENNSYLVANIA

77TH REGIMENT INFANTRY
5TH BRIGADE (KIRK'S)
2D DIVISION (McCOOK'S)
ARMY OF THE OHIO

ORGANIZED AUGUST 1, 1861 · DISCHARGED JANUARY 16, 1866

# THE PENINSULAR CAMPAIGN

*Cold Harbor National Cemetery, where thousands of Union soldiers who died in the Peninsular Campaign are buried. Dogtags were not yet standard issue during the Civil War, and the majority of soldiers killed in action were unidentified, like this man.*

(Previous page) *Boatswain's Creek, at the Gaines's Mill Battlefield, is typical of the swampy lowlands in which Confederate Generals Johnston and Lee forced Maj. Gen. George B. McClellan's Army of the Potomac to fight.*

I n the months following the First Battle of Bull Run, fighting in the east ground to a halt while the North prepared itself for all-out war. During this time the Federal troops around Washington, D.C., were strengthened by an influx of volunteers who signed on for three years rather than the 90 days that had marked the war's first troop enlistments. These soldiers were reorganized into the fighting force that would eventually win the war in the east: the Army of the Potomac.

In August 1861 this new army was placed under the command of a young major general named George Brinton McClellan. McClellan had been fortunate enough to win a minor victory in western Virginia just before the Union defeat at Bull Run, and he was assigned to the Army of the Potomac as one of the North's few successful generals. A master organizer, he began carefully molding his troops into well-trained fighting men. Day after day, privates and officers alike were thoroughly drilled in the tactics and maneuvers they would need when they faced the enemy again. After several months, the high command was getting anxious to see all of this drilling and parading put to work, but McClellan—demonstrating for the first time the overcautious slowness which was to characterize his command—kept insisting that his army was not yet ready for battle. President Lincoln finally had to order McClellan to fight, and in March 1862 the Army of the Potomac entered the war.

The massive campaign that McClellan planned would more than justify the army's months of training...if it worked. McClellan's plan was to send 90,000 men—all the troops under his command except those assigned to the defense of Washington—to the peninsula between the York and James Rivers in Virginia. The objective was to capture the Confederate capital of Richmond and thereby discredit the Southern government. The troops would sail to Fort Monroe, a U.S. Army toehold on the tip of the peninsula,

*This was Union commander George B. McClellan's goal: the Confederate capitol building in Richmond, Virginia. (Library of Congress)*

This Confederate cavalryman is typical of Jeb Stuart's horsemen, with a well-polished saber (right) and high-topped boots. Unlike Union troopers, Confederate cavalrymen provided their own horses and tack.

southeast of Richmond. From there they would march overland some 100 miles to the Confederate capital and lay siege to the city.

The Federal troops arrived at Fort Monroe without incident and began their advance westward on April 4, 1862. Their first objective was Yorktown, on the north side the peninsula; the rebel artillery there controlled the York River, and McClellan wanted the York freed to use as his supply route. Convinced by faulty military intelligence that he faced an army of 120,000 men at Yorktown, McClellan decided that his 90,000 men could only capture the town by bombarding it into submission. (In fact, the force there was much smaller than his own—about 55,000 men under Gen. Joseph E. Johnston—and the Union army could probably have stormed the town.) The Federals wasted a month placing huge artillery pieces around Yorktown only to have the Confederates there depart for Richmond on May 3 without a shot being fired. (McClellan's gun emplacements are still visible in the Yorktown Battlefield Park.) The Yankees caught up with Johnston's rear guard at Williamsburg, Virginia, on May 5 and engaged them in some costly fighting, but the Federal forces were unable to stop the Confederates from reaching their new base of operations at Richmond.

With Johnston's army in the Confederate capital, there was nothing left on the peninsula to hinder McClellan's advance except the Virginia mud, and the Army of the Potomac continued its ponderous march westward. By the end of May the Yankees had moved into place east of Richmond, their lines extending 15 miles north and south of the Chickahominy River, which runs down the middle of the peninsula there. The Army of the Potomac was close enough to Richmond to hear the city's church bells, and the only thing preventing it from

*Beaver Dam Creek, seen here, was the site of the first of the Seven Days' Battles that drove McClellan's Yankees from the outskirts of Richmond.*

51

*Gen. Robert E. Lee, who was appointed Confederate commander of the Army of Northern Virginia on June 1, 1862, prior to the Peninsular Campaign's Seven Days' Battles.*

*Gen. Robert E. Lee, seen here with his son George Washington Custis Lee (left) and Col. Walter Taylor. (Library of Congress)*

attacking the Confederate capital at that point was its commanding general's imagination. McClellan firmly believed that the Confederates had more than 160,000 soldiers facing him and that his army—now reinforced to over 100,000 men—needed even more troops before he could attack Richmond; in reality, the city was defended by fewer than 70,000 soldiers.

McClellan's wait for more troops was to prove costly. After heavy rains on May 30, Confederate General Johnston decided to attack McClellan's forces south of the Chickahominy, knowing that the riverbanks would be flooded into a swampy morass which would prevent the Yankees from consolidating their superior numbers against him. Although the Confederate attack at the Battle of Seven Pines (or

Fair Oaks) on May 31, 1862, was not decisive, the heavy fighting there had two important consequences: it bolstered McClellan's fears, forestalling any further Federal advances; and it saw the wounded Joseph Johnston replaced as the Confederate commander by a man who would soon become a legend: Gen. Robert E. Lee.

Lee—a highly respected officer and brilliant strategist who had been serving as Jefferson Davis's chief military adviser—christened his new command the Army of Northern Virginia and immediately began formulating one of the daring offensive plans which became his trademark during the war. He put his men to work improving Richmond's defenses so the city could be held with far fewer soldiers, and he sent word to Stonewall Jackson to bring over his 20,000 troops, who had been marching rings around the Union forces in the Shenandoah Valley. Lee also detailed his dashing young cavalry commander, Brig. Gen.

*One of the cannon which drove the attacking rebels from Malvern Hill, saving McClellan's retreating army in the last of the Seven Days' Battles.*

APPROXIMATE LINE OF
WHITING'S ADVANCE
NEAR THIS POINT, BETWEEN THE BRIGADES OF
MARTINDALE AND BUTTERFIELD, CONFEDERATE FORCES
FIRST PENETRATED THE MAIN FEDERAL POSITION
IN THE BATTLE OF GAINES' MILL, JUNE 27, 1862.
THE FOURTH TEXAS REGIMENT LED THE CHARGE.

(Opposite) *Here, near the center of the Federal line, Lee's Confederates broke through the Union defenses at Gaines's Mill after five hours of desperate fighting.*

James Ewell Brown (Jeb) Stuart, to make a reconnaissance of the Yankee lines. In a typically spectacular maneuver, Stuart's men rode 150 miles around McClellan's entire army, gathering much valuable information and humiliating the Union command by eluding capture.

By June 25, 1862, Lee was ready to fight, in the first of what would be known as the Seven Days' Battles. He left the defenses of Richmond to a skeleton force of 27,000 and moved every other man he had, 60,000 in all—including Jackson's men just in from the Shenandoah—8 miles northeast of Richmond to attack the right end of McClellan's line at Beaver Dam Creek (now part of the Richmond Battlefield Park, near Mechanicsville,

Virginia). Stonewall Jackson was to circle his men north of the Yankee position and attack it from the east, while troops under Maj. Gen. James C. Longstreet and Maj. Gen. Ambrose P. Hill moved in from the west, at Chickahominy Bluffs.

By noon of June 26, Jackson's men—perhaps exhausted from their recent campaign in the Shenandoah—had not yet attacked, and General Hill decided to move forward on his own. The Federal position at Beaver Dam Creek was strong and Hill failed to capture it, but the attack led the fearful McClellan to pull back the troops from Beaver Dam anyway. They reformed at an even better defensive position a few miles to the east near Gaines's Mill (a Richmond Battlefield sit on the north side of the Chickahominy River). Lee attacked there on June 27, and in desperate fighting drove the Union troops south of the Chickahominy.

Stunned by this Confederate offensive, McClellan, who was now convinced that Lee's army totaled 200,000 men, decided to abandon his Richmond campaign and retreat to the safety of the U.S. Navy gunboats moored in the James River at Harrison's Landing on the south side of the peninsula. He moved out on June 28, 1862, burning the bridges over the Chickahominy behind him to slow Lee's pursuit. The Army of Northern Virginia could not circle around the Yankees fast enough to block their

*Brig. Gen. James Ewell Brown (Jeb) Stuart, Lee's youthful cavalry commander, led a daring reconnaissance ride around McClellan's entire army before the Seven Days' Battles.*

*A close-up of the monument to Stonewall Jackson in Richmond, Virginia. Lee called upon his most trusted general to come from the Shenandoah Valley to aid in the Seven Days' Battles.*

retreat, but they harassed the Union march south with battles at Savage Station on June 29 and Frayser's Farm (White Oak Swamp) on June 30. On July 1, Lee tried one last assault on the Union army at Malvern Hill, another Richmond Battlefield site today, just north of Harrison's Landing. The Federal position on the hill was too well secured for the rebels to storm, however, and the Union artillery there repelled the Confederates with heavy casualties. The next day the Army of the Potomac pulled back to its new base at Harrisons's Landing. George McClellan's plan to capture the Confederate capital was thwarted. Robert E. Lee's resourceful leadership in the Seven Days' Battles had saved Richmond...and the Confederacy.

*Confederate President Jefferson Davis, seen here in a bronze statue in Richmond, Virginia, saw his capital saved from capture by the brilliant strategy of his military adviser, Gen. Robert E. Lee.*

# SECOND
# BULL RUN

Although Gen. Robert E. Lee's Army of Northern Virginia had driven the Federal troops from Richmond in June 1862, as of late July the Confederate capital remained in a precarious situation. Maj. Gen. George B. McClellan's 100,000 Yankees were still just 18 miles away in their camp on the peninsula east of Richmond, a potentially deadly threat to Lee's badly outnumbered forces. To make matters worse for the Confederates, another 65,000 Union troops under Maj. Gen. John Pope were marching toward Richmond from Washington, D.C. Faced with the possibility of being trapped between these two Northern armies, Lee developed a daring but risky plan. Leaving a small force to guard the Southern capital, he decided to send his army northward to battle Pope closer to Washington, gambling that the Lincoln administration—always concerned with safeguarding the U.S. capital—would then pull McClellan's troops off the peninsula and back to Washington. If Lee was correct, he would thus eliminate both Federal threats to Richmond at the same time. But the campaign required precise timing in order to be successful. If Lee could not defeat Pope soon after the Yankees had been decoyed from the peninsula, McClellan would have time to reinforce the embattled army and their combined forces could easily crush Lee's smaller force, destroying the Confederacy's hopes for independence in the process.

In early August, Lee put his plan into operation, sending Maj. Gen. Stonewall Jackson's 24,000 troops from Richmond to seek out Pope's army to the north. On August 9, Jackson en-

*The view from Henry House Hill, where the Union army made its final stand against Maj. Gen. James C. Longstreet's troops on the afternoon of August 30, 1862.*

(Previous page) *Buck Hill, the site of Union Maj. Gen. John Pope's headquarters, east of the army's position on Dogan Ridge.*

*This marker commemorates the site of Jackson's initial engagement in the Second Battle of Bull Run, fought at Groveton on the evening of August 28, 1862.*

countered and defeated the Yankees' lead units under Maj. Gen. Nathaniel P. Banks at Cedar Mountain, Virginia, 70 miles northwest of Richmond, and forced them to retreat to Pope's main line near Culpeper, a few miles to the north. Following this Confederate offensive, the Federal high command ordered McClellan's army to leave the peninsula and sail back to Washington just as Lee had predicted. He had read the Lincoln administration perfectly.

With McClellan heading northward, Lee knew he had to deal with Pope quickly. The Confederate commander left the defenses of Richmond to a handfull of troops and took the rest of his army, 31,000 men under Lt. Gen. James C. Longstreet, to join with Jackson near Cedar Mountain. Lee hoped his total force of 55,000 would be able to rout Pope's army of 65,000 but, by August 22, he had not been able to discover any weakness in Pope's lines where he could mount an attack. Concerned that McClellan would soon be coming to Pope's assistance, Lee again divided his army on August 25, sending Jackson's men on a lightning quick march to the northwest, around Pope's forces. While Longstreet's rebels kept the Yankees near Culpeper occupied, Jackson circled behind them to get his troops between Pope and Washington, D.C. Once the rebels arrived near the Federal capital, Lee reasoned, Pope would be forced to abandon his march toward Richmond and go northward in search of the rebels who, in turn, could lure him into fighting on a site of their choosing, where they would have the advantage.

In just two days Jackson's troops marched 50 miles from Cedar Mountain to Manassas, the site of the Federal army supply depot. Tired and hungry after their Herculean effort, they wasted no time in helping themselves to the huge amounts of food they found. After torching everything that remained, Jackson's men marched off to Groveton, which lay a few miles to the north beyond the First Bull Run (or Manassas) bat-

*Maj. Gen. (later Lt. Gen.) James C. Long-street, one of Lee's most trusted officers, whose troops routed the Yankees at Second Bull Run. (Library of Congress)*

*The Stone House on Warrenton Turnpike served as a hospital during both Battles of Bull Run. Civil War field hospitals were located in houses, barns, and other buildings when available; more often, they were established outdoors.*

tlefield. There, they hid in a deep wood north of the Warrenton Turnpike, which ran east–west through Groveton, to wait for Pope's arrival.

Jackson's raid on Manassas had just the effect that Lee desired. The administration in Washington went into a panic, and Pope's army was dispatched north to intercept the marauding rebels. As soon as Pope began pulling out of Culpeper, Lee and Longstreet left Cedar Mountain, in the hope of rendezvousing with Jackson at Groveton on August 29.

Counting on Lee's arrival the next day, Jackson began the Second Battle of Bull Run late on August 28, attacking a column of Brig. Gen. John Gibbon's famed "Iron Brigade" of hard-fighting westerners as they marched past the rebel hiding place on the Warrenton Turnpike. The brief but heated clash was designed solely to draw Pope into attacking Jackson the following day at an excellent defensive position that had been established in the embankments of an unfinished railroad line, east of Jackson's position in the woods. Pope swallowed the bait. By the morning of August 29, he had gathered most of his 62,000-man army near Dogan Ridge, a mile east of Groveton and half a mile north of the Warrenton Turnpike. Jackson's troops in the railroad cut waited for them about three-quarters of a mile to the northwest.

Pope commenced his attack early on the 29th, assaulting the left end of

(Above right) *The L. Dogan House on Warrenton Turnpike, seen here, was the last remaining wartime structure in the village of Groveton. Longstreet's Confederates drove the retreating Federals past here toward Chinn Ridge to the southeast.*

(Right) *The Deep Cut, scene of the main Union assault on the morning of August 30. This monument, along with the First Bull Run marker at Henry House Hill, was dedicated within weeks of the war's end.*

(Opposite) *The unfinished railroad cut from which Stonewall Jackson's soldiers drove back repeated assaults by Pope's Yankees on August 29 and 30.*

the Confederate defenses with almost 50,000 of his soldiers. But each time some of the charging Yankees made it to the railroad line, Jackson's men, firmly entrenched behind their earthworks, pushed the Federals back with heavy casualties. Afraid to risk his army in one massive assault, Pope foolishly sent in his units piecemeal and, as a result, repeatedly failed to take Jackson's position despite his overwhelming superiority in troops.

Things might have gone differently if the second wing of Pope's army—10,000 men under Maj. Gen. Fitz-John Porter—had attacked the right of the rebel line as Pope had intended. However, the Union commander's orders were apparently unclear to Porter, and he failed to get his troops into the proper position until late in the day, thus giving Longstreet's columns enough time to complete their march from Cedar Mountain and reinforce Jackson. Porter's delay cost the Union army its numerical advantage, and his dereliction earned him a subsequent court-martial (in January 1863 he was cashiered and dismissed from the U.S. Army).

Longstreet's troops, tired after their long march, did not attack on the 29th, and the first day's fighting wound down. That night the Confederates adjusted their lines. Pope misinterpreted their movements as a retreat and on the morning of August 30, convinced that Lee had left, ordered his troops forward around noontime.

The Yankees were stunned by the unexpected gunfire which met them at the railroad embankment; they regrouped and pressed the attack on Jackson's line at the "Deep Cut," an especially steep section of the railroad embankment a little to the west of the first day's fighting. After a couple of hours, Stonewall's Confederates, exhausted and almost out of ammunition, were pushed out of the railroad cut. In response to Jackson's request for help, Longstreet's troops smashed into the left side of the Federal line, driving the Yankees from the field.

Pope's soldiers quickly retreated to the southeast across the Warrenton Turnpike, holding off Longstreet's

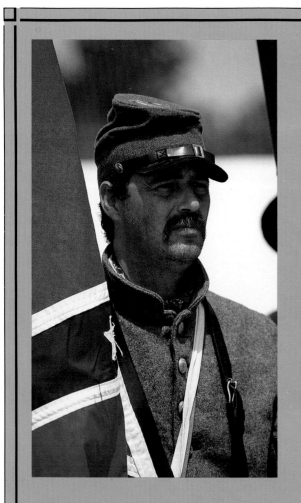

Lee's soldiers, well equipped and near the peak of their strength at the time of Second Bull Run, looked much like the gray-clad Confederate colorbearer at left. The Southerners in the field wore a wide variety of clothing, as seen in the skirmishing unit above. Straw hats, butternut-dyed jackets (such as that worn by the man kneeling at center left)—even captured Union blue trousers and coats—were more common among enlisted men than the all-gray uniforms typically associated with the Confederacy today.

men as best they could. At one spot—now marked by the battlefield's New York monuments—the famous 5th New York Duryee Zouaves and the 10th New York National Zouaves took a heroic but futile stand against the Confederate attack, and in five minutes the Fifth lost 123 men. Other Union units fought farther to the east at Chinn Ridge, delaying Longstreet's attack long enough for Pope to establish a final line of defense behind them at Henry House Hill, the site of some of the hardest fighting at the First Battle of Bull Run. Here, the Union army was able to fend off the Confederates

until dusk, when the fighting ended. That night, Pope's army retreated toward Washington.

The Federal defeat at the Second Battle of Bull Run cost the Union 16,000 men and opened the door for Lee to move his army northward, carrying the war into Maryland and the Antietam campaign. It also cost Pope his command. The ineffectual general was sent to the Northwest to fight Indians, and his former troops in Virginia were reassigned to George McClellan's Army of the Potomac.

*This monument honors the Fifth New York Volunteers, who lost 123 soldiers while holding back Longstreet's attack on August 30. This was the highest fatality rate of any regiment during a single battle of the war.*

The foundation of the Chinn family home, on the southwestern end of Chinn Ridge. Union troops were driven here by Longstreet's attack on August 30.

A detail of the Chinn House foundation.

ANTIETAM

*The youthful face of this infantryman on the monument to the 130th Pennsylvania Regiment reflects the tender age of most soldiers who donned the blue and gray.*

(Previous page) *The Army of the Potomac's commitment to repelling Lee's northern invasion is embodied in this stern-faced statue at the Cornfield.*

(Opposite) *The Mumma family cemetery, adjacent to the Mumma farm site near the East Woods. The farm buildings were burned during the battle to prevent their use by Union sharpshooters.*

Robert E. Lee saw a perfect opportunity to move his army north after the Second Battle of Bull Run. With John Pope's army defeated and George McClellan's Army of the Potomac not yet back on its feet after the Peninsular Campaign, the Confederates could advance into Maryland and Pennsylvania unimpeded. Lee and Confederate President Jefferson Davis had several reasons for undertaking a Northern invasion: first, it would carry the war out of Virginia, which had borne the brunt of the fighting in the east; second, it would encourage the border state of Maryland to join the Confederacy; and, third, if a military victory could be won, it would embarrass the North on its own territory and bolster the Confederate States' case for recognition as an independent nation by Britain and France.

Lee's Army of Northern Virginia moved out of the Manassas area on September 3, 1862. The 50,000 Confederates crossed the Potomac into Maryland on September 4 and headed to Frederick, Maryland, where Lee split his forces for a surprise attack on the Federal arsenal at Harper's Ferry 18 miles to the southwest. On September 9, Lee ordered 30,000 troops under Maj. Gen. Stonewall Jackson, Maj. Gen. Lafayette McLaws, and Brig. Gen. John G. Walker to seize Harper's Ferry while Lee remained with the rest of Lt. Gen. James C. Longstreet's command west of Frederick at South Mountain to plan his next move.

Lee divided his army confident that the Federals would not be ready to pursue him for some time. For once, though, McClellan moved quickly, leading more than 70,000 soldiers out of Washington on September 7. They arrived at Frederick on the 12th, skirmishing with the Confederates at South Mountain on the 14th and driving them to the west, toward the Potomac River. At this point Lee considered abandoning his Maryland

*Maj. Gen. George B. McClellan, commander of the Federal Army of the Potomac. A brilliant organizer, ''Little Mac'' proved too slow for field command. (Library of Congress)*

campaign and returning to Virginia. He had fewer than 20,000 soldiers at South Mountain to face McClellan's 70,000, and with his back to the Potomac River he had few routes of escape should the Yankees attack him in force. Just as Lee was weighing his options, however, Stonewall Jackson notified him that Harper's Ferry would probably surrender on September 15 and that most of Jackson's troops would be able to join Lee afterward. Lee then decided to make a stand at Sharpsburg, Maryland, situated between the Potomac River and Antietam Creek about 7 miles north of Harper's Ferry and 10 miles southwest of South Mountain.

Lee began assembling Longstreet's soldiers at Sharpsburg on September 15 and finished the placement of his forces when Jackson's 20,000 troops arrived from Harper's Ferry the next day. Lee posted the Confederates north and east of Sharpsburg on a line running from the Potomac River on the west to the Antietam Creek, ending at the southernmost of three bridges which spanned the stream in that vicinity. One major roadway, the Hagerstown Pike—connecting Sharpsburg and Hagerstown, Maryland—ran north–south down the center of the Confederate lines.

McClellan's 70,000 soldiers arrived on the field early on September 16. He could no doubt have crushed Longstreet's army of 20,000 if he had attacked promptly, but the Union commander—believing, once again, that the Southern forces outnumbered his—had returned to his overcautious slowness, giving Stonewall Jackson's troops enough time to join with Long-

*The Dunker Church. The original building was destroyed in a storm in 1921; this replica was constructed in 1962.*

*(Opposite) The Georgian Memorial at Antietam. Georgia had more units at the battle than any other Confederate state except Virginia.*

street's. McClellan took a full day to get his troops into position, deploying them on both sides of Antietam Creek east of Sharpsburg. The Union line began at the Hagerstown Pike on the north and extended southward to the bridge which anchored the Confederate line.

McClellan opened his attack from the north on the morning of September 17, sending troops under Brig. Gen. Joseph Hooker south along the Hagerstown Pike toward a small church of the German Dunker sect

about a mile away. Hooker's men moved out around 6 a.m., first encountering Jackson's force in a cornfield to the east of the Pike. The fighting here was fierce, and the Union troops were mowed down in rows as they marched; but the Federals pressed on, pushing the outnumbered Confederates into the "West Woods" just north of the Dunker Church.

More Union troops were sent in from the northeast to support Hooker around 7 a.m., moving through the "East Woods" beside the cornfield. Their commander, Brig. Gen. Joseph K. F. Mansfield, was under the mistaken impression that Union forces held these woods and marched his troops into a Confederate surprise attack which killed hundreds of men. Mansfield himself was fatally wounded, dying the next day. His forces regrouped, however, and cleared the rebels out of the East Woods, forcing them from the cornfield as well. Mansfield's troops eventually fought their way to the West Woods, where they hung on tenuously, waiting for reinforcements.

As Mansfield's soldiers were pushing toward the West Woods, more Federal troops under Brig. Gen. John Sedg-

wick were moving in from the east. Stonewall Jackson's forces were hard pressed to meet this latest assault, and just as it seemed their line would break—around 10:30 a.m.—McLaws's Confederates came roaring in from Harper's Ferry. Sedgwick's Yankees marched right into them, and in half an hour of withering fire, 2200 Federal troops were killed or wounded. The remainder of Sedgwick's forces— along with the remnants of Mansfield's and Hooker's commands—retreated to the safety of the Federal artillery to the north, and the fighting on the north end of the battlefield ended around 11:30 a.m. The battle had already cost 6000 Confederate and 7000 Yankee casualties.

About the time that Sedgwick's soldiers were moving toward the West Woods, the focus of the battle shifted to a low, curving path running to the east of the Hagerstown Pike at a point southeast of the Dunker Church. Here, at what would ever after be known as "Bloody Lane," Union forces under Brig. Gen. William H. French pushed southward, fighting

*Confederate dead lie next to the Hagerstown Pike (right) near the Cornfield, just a few of the casualties from America's bloodiest day of fighting. (Library of Congress)*

*This rocky ground south of the Cornfield changed hands several times during the three and a half hours that Yankees and Southerners vied for control of the northern end of the battlefield.*

The 104th New York Regiment, which was raised in the vicinity of Albany, the state capital, lost more than 80 men in the Cornfield, where this memorial is located.

Looking north from the Confederate lines toward Bloody Lane, scene of the midday fighting. The tall structure in the left background is a battlefield observation tower.

The Federal fighting man as he would have appeared during the Antietam campaign. He wears a loose-fitting ''bummer'' cap and four-button sack coat rather than a full-dress uniform. The straps across his chest support his canteen, cartridge box, and haversack, which held his rations on the march.

furiously with Longstreet's troops. For three hours artillerymen and foot-soldiers fired back and forth, exacting a total of 6000 casualties on both sides. Finally, at around 1 p.m., the Yankees secured Bloody Lane and the fields surrounding it, and the badly battered Confederates moved back to their defensive lines near Sharpsburg.

As the combat at Bloody Lane was reaching its peak, General Lee was forced to move troops into the heart of the battle from the southern end of his line, leaving only a few hundred soldiers to hold the bridge over Antietam Creek there. If the U.S. troops posted on the other side of the creek had moved forward at that time they could have rolled right over Lee's army, but the Union commander, Maj. Gen. Ambrose E. Burnside, ignored repeated orders to attack all morning. When he finally got his troops into action around 1 p.m. he concentrated all his efforts on capturing the bridge (now called Burnside Bridge, a major battlefield landmark), erroneously convinced that it was the only route over the easily waded Antietam. It was close to 3 o'clock by the time he got his 13,000 men across the creek and began moving them toward Lee's lines.

The Yankees might still have over-come the Army of Northern Virginia except for the timely arrival of the last of Jackson's troops from Harper's Ferry. Lt. Gen. Ambrose P. Hill's men had just finished mopping-up opera-tions there that morning and marched on the double-quick to Sharpsburg, arriving about 4 p.m. Although his 3000 soldiers were nearly exhausted and heavily outnumbered by Burn-side's men, Hill's troops unexpectedly crashed into the Yankee line near the bridge with a force that drove the Northern troops back. The sudden appearance of Hill's men convinced McClellan that Lee had more troops than did the Army of the Potomac.

*Antietam's Clara Barton Monument salutes the volunteer nurse who came to Antietam with badly needed food and medical supplies. After the war she organized the American Red Cross to carry on relief work.*

(Opposite) *Burnside Bridge, at the southeast corner of the battlefield. Union Maj. Gen. Ambrose E. Burnside wasted two hours capturing this span across the easily forded Antietam Creek.*

*President Lincoln conferring with McClellan two weeks after the Battle of Antietam. Dissatisfied with the general's leadership, Lincoln removed him from command shortly thereafter. (Library of Congress)*

Fearing defeat from an overwhelming enemy, the Union commander called off the attack and the day's combat ceased.

The Battle of Antietam was the bloodiest single day of fighting in the Civil War, with more than 12,000 Union and 10,000 Confederate casualties, but it decided little. The engagement ended in a stalemate, and McClellan allowed Lee's army to recross the Potomac into Virginia unmolested.

The major result of the battle was political rather than military. Although Antietam was not a Northern victory, neither was it another Union defeat; and following the display of Federal force at Antietam, President Lincoln felt justified in issuing his famous Emancipation Proclamation, which as of January 1, 1863, freed the slaves in all of the states in rebellion against the United States. Lincoln knew that the Proclamation would be seen as empty verbiage without first some demonstration of Union strength, and Antietam gave him that demonstration. The Proclamation, which made the North's fight a battle against slavery as well as a struggle to preserve the Union, identified the South as a force upholding human slavery, effectively blocking recognition of the Confederacy by European powers which had themselves outlawed human bondage years before.

FREDERICKSBURG

Robert E. Lee's Army of Northern Virginia returned to the safety of its home soil following the Battle of Antietam in September 1862. The Confederates crossed the Potomac into Virginia at Sharpsburg, Maryland, on September 18 and headed south down the Shenandoah Valley. Lee had Lt. Gen. Stonewall Jackson's troops guard the Shenandoah while Lt. Gen. James C. Longstreet's forces moved into eastern Virginia to establish a new base camp. By November 1862, Longstreet's troops were concentrated near the village of Culpeper Court House, located on the Orange & Alexandria Railroad about 30 miles east of the Shenandoah.

As Jackson and Longstreet's Confederates marched into Virginia, the Union Army of the Potomac, under Maj. Gen. George B. McClellan, followed slowly behind. Ever mindful of protecting the Federal capital, McClellan was careful to place his troops between the Confederates and Washington, D.C. By early November he had the Union army scattered northeast of Culpeper almost to Washington, keeping an eye on the Southerners but taking no action against them. This was the last straw for President Lincoln, who had become thoroughly disgusted with McClellan's lack of aggressiveness. On November 1, 1862, McClellan was dismissed as the commander of the Army of the Potomac.

Lincoln named Maj. Gen. Ambrose E. Burnside as the new commander. Burnside was well meaning and politically acceptable to the Lincoln administration but sadly lacking in the tactical expertise and inherent leadership needed in a commanding

*The National Cemetery at the foot of Marye's Heights is the final resting place for more than 16,000 Federal soldiers who died at the Battles of Fredericksburg, Chancellorsville, the Wilderness, and Spotsylvania.*

*(Previous page) The Pennsylvania volunteers honored by this statue fought valiantly at Fredericksburg, but their efforts were wasted by an inept Federal commander.*

general. Burnside himself was not blind to his shortcomings and did not seek command of the Army of the Potomac, but he accepted it to prevent another general whom he disliked, Joseph Hooker, from getting the position.

Once he had the job, though, Burnside—unlike McClellan—was astute enough to realize that the nation expected its soldiers to fight, so he quickly developed a battle plan for the Army of the Potomac: he would move the Union forces to Falmouth, Virginia, about 30 miles southeast of Lee's position at Culpeper. There, the Yankee soldiers would cross the Rappahannock River into Fredericksburg and sweep on to capture Richmond before Lee had a chance to stop them.

The new Union commander got his troops moving quickly, and on November 17 the first Federal units reached Falmouth. They arrived before General Lee knew where they were headed, and things briefly looked good for the Army of the Potomac; but the portable pontoon bridges which Burnside felt he needed to cross the Rappahannock had not yet been sent from Washington, and the unimaginative Union general had his men wait at Falmouth until the bridges arrived. While the Yankees were waiting, Lee had time to summon Stonewall Jackson's soldiers from the Shenandoah Valley and send them, along with Longstreet's troops at Culpeper, to Fredericksburg.

When Burnside's engineers were finally ready to build their pontoon bridges across the Rappahannock in December, the Fredericksburg area was firmly held by the Confederates. Lee had 1600 men in the town to hold off the Army of the Potomac's crossing, and he placed the rest of his forces—more than 70,000 men—on the high ground west of Fredericksburg about a mile from the Rappahannock. (The river flows in a southerly direc-

At left, a Confederate infantryman repairs his percussion-cap rifle, shown above in a detail from the New Jersey Monument. The standard weapon of the Civil War infantryman, it was much more accurate and reliable than the flintlock muskets used in earlier wars. These guns were loaded in several steps. First, a premeasured charge of black powder and a conical lead bullet were rammed down the muzzle of the barrel. Then, the soldier placed a small copper cap containing a mild explosive on the tube leading from the lock to the end of the barrel (covered here by the soldier's wrench). When the rifle's trigger was pulled, the hammer (left) hit the cap, which sent a hot spark down the tube and ignited the powder. A soldier could fire two or three shots a minute.

tion between Falmouth and Fredericks-burg, so that the town is actually on the Rappahannock's western bank.) When Burnside's troops started assembling their bridges on the morning of December 11, the Confederate sharpshooters in Fredericksburg began picking them off and Federal soldiers had to be sent over to the town by boat to clear the area of snipers. By the morning of December 12, however, the Union engineers had completed six bridges across the Rappahannock, three opposite Fredericksburg and three about a half mile downstream to the south.

Burnside got most of his troops across these two river crossings early on the 12th. Instead of attacking at once, though, the Union commander spent a day getting his units into position for a two-pronged offensive concentrated at Fredericksburg and the Yankees' downstream crossing. This delay allowed the Confederate commanders to discern the Union battle plan and move their defenses accor-

*Two of the pontoon bridges which Burnside's Yankees used to cross the Rappahannock River below Fredericksburg. (Library of Congress)*

*This statue honors Richard Kirkland, known as the ''Angel of Marye's Heights,'' a Confederate sergeant who risked his life to bring water to the Union wounded in front of the stone wall on the morning of December 14, 1862.*

*The deadly stone wall on Marye's Heights, goal of General Burnside's fruitless assaults on December 13. (Library of Congress)*

*The stone wall as it appears on the battlefield today.*

dingly. Lee placed Longstreet's men a half mile west of the city of Fredericksburg on a sharp ridge called Marye's Heights (so named because it ran in front of Brompton, the Marye family home). Stonewall Jackson's troops were placed on the hills south of Marye's Heights, facing the Yankees' downstream bridges.

The Federal assault was finally launched on the morning of December 13, with the troops at the downstream crossing leading the attack around 11 o'clock. The commander of those Union troops, Maj. Gen. William B. Franklin, assumed that Burnside would have his 46,000 men attempt to dislodge Jackson's forces from the hills south of Marye's Heights—the only move on that front that made tactical sense for the Union army—and had drafted orders for such an attack. Burnside countermanded these orders, however, and instructed Franklin to hold a strategically unimportant road in front of Jackson's position instead. Despite Franklin's protests, the Union commander inexplicably permitted only 4500 of Franklin's men, just one-tenth of his command, to attack Jackson's troops on the hills. These 4500 men under Maj. Gen. George Gordon Meade—whose leadership is commemorated with a monument at this part of the battlefield—fought well and managed to break through the Confederate lines at a spot that is now on the Battlefield Park's Lee Drive. Meade's success was short-lived, though. Unsupported by reinforcements, his men could not maintain their position and were forced back to Franklin's lines around 2 p.m. This concluded the Federal fighting on this part of the battlefield, and Franklin's troops remained idle for the rest of the day.

As Meade was fruitlessly fighting his way into the Confederate lines southwest of town, an even more disastrous Union assault was taking place west of Fredericksburg. General Burnside had the Federal troops there attempting to storm the Confederate position on Marye's Heights, a half mile across an open plain from the streets of Fredericksburg. Initially, the

*Chatham Manor, across the river from Fredericksburg, was the headquarters for Union Maj. Gen. Edwin V. Sumner during the battle. This 18th-century mansion is the only building known to have been visited by both George Washington and Abraham Lincoln.*

*The view from Confederate Brig. Gen. John B. Hood's line, on the ridge south of Marye's Heights.*

advancing Yankees were battered by Confederate artillery fire. Then, as they approached the crest of the Heights, they were met with a murderous volley of gunfire from Longstreet's troops, who were entrenched behind a stone wall at the summit (now a central feature of the National Battlefield). As one line of riflemen fired at the Yankees, several other lines of infantry loaded their single-shot rifles and passed them forward to the marksmen at the wall. In this way they were able to keep up an unceasing hail of bullets every bit as

effective as a machine gun, decimating the approaching Federal troops. Unit after unit was cut down as it marched, including the Union's famed Irish Brigade, made up of hard-fighting Irish immigrants who were determined to prove their loyalty to their new homeland; but Burnside—who remained in his headquarters across the river at Falmouth and did not witness the carnage—refused to call off the attack or change his battle plan. By nightfall, more than 6000 Union soldiers had perished before Marye's Heights in the most senseless slaughter of the war. None had made it any closer than 100 feet to the Confederates' deadly stone wall.

Incredibly, Burnside attempted to continue the fight at Marye's Heights the following day. During the night of December 13, he sent fresh troops

across the plain to a small rise about 300 feet from the wall, but the next morning they were discovered and pinned down by Confederate fire. Unable to move, they stayed hidden behind the rise all day, returning to the Federal lines on the evening of December 14 without having fired a shot. After this, Burnside's senior commanders refused to risk any more lives in such useless attacks. Defeated in the most ill-conceived Union battle of the war, the Army of the Potomac retreated across the Rappahannock on the evening of December 15, 1862, pulling up its bridges behind it.

# CHANCELLORSVILLE

*An artillery caisson and limber at Fairview. The limber (right) holds one ammunition chest; the caisson, two ammunition chests and spare parts. Each cannon had its own caisson and limber.*

*(Previous page) An artillery piece at Chancellorsville. The fog recalls the heavy smoke once generated by the gun's black powder.*

The Union's Army of the Potomac spent the winter of 1862/63 in camp at Falmouth, Virginia, following the Battle of Fredericksburg, while Gen. Robert E. Lee's Army of Northern Virginia remained across the Rappahannock near Fredericksburg. For the Army of the Potomac, it was a time to recover from its disastrous defeat in that battle. In January 1863 the Army received a new commander, Maj. Gen. Joseph Hooker, who succeeded the hapless Burnside. Hooker was a bit of a braggart and his attitude rubbed many of his fellow generals the wrong way, but he had a solid reputation as a fighting man (he was nicknamed "Fighting Joe" by the Northern press) and President Lincoln hoped he would be the aggressive leader the North needed. Hooker saw

to it that his men were well rested that winter and reinforced the Army with new recruits, swelling its ranks to 130,000 men; by the spring of 1863 it was once again ready for action.

General Hooker developed a battle plan that reflected his nickname. Leaving 60,000 troops at Falmouth to decoy General Lee, he planned to lead 70,000 Union soldiers around Lee's lines and swoop down on the Confederates in Fredericksburg from the west. The new Union commander got this campaign underway on April 27, 1863, sending his lead units to the north and west, carefully screened from Confederate observers in Fredericksburg. Crossing the Rappahannock more than 20 miles upstream at a place called Kelly's Ford, they swung to the southeast and marched by different routes to a tiny crossroads village called Chancellorsville, about 10 miles west of Fredericksburg. While these units were en route, the Union troops still stationed in Falmouth placed pontoon bridges across the Rappahannock south of Fredericksburg and created a diversion on Lee's front to draw the Confederate commander's attention away from the west, where the real Federal attack would occur.

The Yankees' march to Chancellorsville went perfectly, and on April 30 the last of Hooker's 70,000 assault troops arrived there. Chancellorsville was an excellent moving-off point for Hooker's attack on Fredericksburg. It lay near the eastern edge of the "Wilderness"—an area of dense forest and heavy underbrush to the west of Fredericksburg—and was thus well hidden from Lee's army. Chancellorsville also lay at the junction of three roads which led to Fredericksburg: the Orange Turnpike, which ran eastward through Chancellorsville to Fredericksburg; the Orange Plank Road, which looped southeast from the turnpike in Chancellorsville, curving north to rejoin the turnpike about 5 miles to the east; and the River Road, which went north from Chancellorsville to the Rappahannock River, paralleling the riverbank into Fredericksburg. Hooker planned to use all three roads for his attack on Lee, but until he was ready to attack, the Union commander concentrated his troops on a 3-mile stretch of the Orange Turnpike west of the Chancel-

(Above right) *Maj. Gen. Joseph ("Fighting Joe") Hooker. The Union commander was outgeneraled at Chancellorsville by Lee and Jackson. (Library of Congress)*

*This monument honors Confederate Brig. Gen. Elisha F. Paxton, who was killed in the attack on the Federal center at Fairview on May 3, 1863.*

(Opposite) *The high ground of Fairview east of Hazel Grove. When the Confederate artillery secured Fairview on May 3, the Southerners were able to drive the Yankees from Chancellorsville.*

*Lt. Gen. Thomas J. ("Stonewall") Jackson, who led the surprise Confederate attack against Hooker's right flank at Chancellorsville. That night, Jackson was accidentally shot by his own troops while making a reconnaissance of the Union lines. (Library of Congress)*

*Old Salem Church, on Orange Turnpike, 7 miles east of Chancellorsville. Here, on May 4, Lee's soldiers defeated the last of Hooker's forces from Fredericksburg. Following this, on May 6, the Union army retreated north across the Rappahannock River.*

*The foundation of the Chancellorsville Tavern, which served as Union Maj. Gen. Joseph Hooker's headquarters. During the battle a Confederate artillery shot hit the tavern porch while Hooker was standing there, knocking him senseless.*

lorsville crossroads. Hooker himself made his headquarters at the Chancellorsville Tavern at the crossroads (the foundations of which are still extant and are a major stop for visitors who tour the battlefield).

The Union assault troops' march to Chancellorsville, while well executed, had not gone unnoticed by the Confederates. Maj. Gen. Jeb Stuart's cavalry patrols spotted Federal soldiers gathering near the village on the evening of April 29 and warned General Lee of a possible attack. Lee was in a particularly bad position, for Lt. Gen. James C. Longstreet's troops had been temporarily removed from his command that winter, leaving Lee with only 60,000 men to face Hooker's far larger army. The Confederate commander had only two choices: he could retreat southward, or he could try to outmaneuver Hooker. Typically, Lee opted to go on the offensive and attacked an enemy that outnumbered him two to one in what many military

historians consider to be the most daring and brilliant campaign of the war. On April 30, Lee left about 10,000 Confederate troops to hold Fredericksburg and moved the rest of the Army of Northern Virginia—now fewer than 50,000 men—west to fight Hooker.

By the morning of May 1, 1863, Lee had troops under the command of Maj. Gen. Richard H. Anderson posted north and south across the eastern junction of the Orange Turnpike and Orange Plank Road about 5 miles from Chancellorsville. Anderson's Confederates, supported by Maj. Gen. Lafayette McLaws's troops, began moving west on these two roads around 11 a.m. At the same time, Hooker began the Union army's advance eastward to Fredericksburg along these same routes. The Federal troops, their vision limited by the forest which was supposed to screen them from Lee, unexpectedly collided with the advancing Confederates shortly after noon, stunning Hooker. The Union commander—suddenly losing some of his bravado—ordered a

*This monument marks the spot on the Orange Plank Road where Stonewall Jackson was wounded on the evening of May 2.*

ON THIS SPOT
FELL
MORTALLY WOUNDED
THOMAS J. JACKSON
Lt. Gen. C. S. A.
MAY 2ND 1863.

*Confederate artillery battery at Hazel Grove, between Catharine Forge and the Orange Turnpike. The assault against the Federal center on May 3 began here.*

Cooking in camp. When Stonewall Jackson started his surprise attack on the Union army at Chancellorsville, the Yankees were cooking their evening meals. The meager field rations for soldiers on both sides were the same: hard bread or corn meal, greasy salt pork, and coffee. Vegetables of any sort—fresh or dried—were a rarity.

retreat back to Chancellorsville, establishing defensive lines along the Orange Turnpike extending 3 miles west of the village and 1 mile to the east.

Lee's scouts discovered that the eastern end of Hooker's line was too well defended to attack but the western end was wide open for assault. On hearing this, Lee met with Lt. Gen. Stonewall Jackson on the night of May 1—at what the battlefield park now calls the "Lee–Jackson Bivouac" site. There the two Confederate generals planned an audacious attack on the western flank of the Army of the Potomac. Lee decided to divide his already meager forces yet again, holding back Hooker's eastern flank with just 18,000 men while Jackson circled around Hooker's western flank with 28,000 soldiers.

Jackson's troops left on their 12-mile march at 7:30 on the morning of May 2, heading southwest from the Orange Plank Road along some backwoods paths now identified as the battlefield park's Furnace Road and Jackson Trail East. They turned to the northwest along what is now called

Jackson Trail West midway in their march. The Confederate column was spotted near Catharine Furnace—an old ironworks at the intersection of Furnace Road and Jackson Trail East a mile south of Hooker's center on the Orange Turnpike. Jackson's rear guard was captured by Union Maj. Gen. Daniel E. Sickles's troops around 1 p.m., but Hooker was unconcerned by the Southern troop movement on his front, assuming that the Confederates were merely retreating.

Jackson's troops arrived at the Orange Turnpike west of the Union lines around 5 p.m. on May 2 and immediately formed for attack. The Southern force swarmed out of the woods into the Federal camp just as the Union soldiers—part of Maj. Gen. Oliver O. Howard's command—were preparing their evening meal. Caught totally by surprise, the Federals ran eastward toward Chancellorsville in utter chaos, not stopping until they reached the safety of the Union lines east of town. Once the Yankee rout was halted on the evening of May 2,

*This marker indicates the trenches dug near Catharine Furnace by Brig. Gen. Carnot Posey's Confederates, part of Maj. Gen. Richard H. Anderson's command.*

the Federal commanders established a defensive line running north and south of the Chancellorsville crossroads from Catharine Forge to the Rappahannock River and awaited the rebels' next move.

General Lee—his Army still heavily outnumbered by the Yankees—was anxious to press his advantage while he could. He attacked again on May 3, advancing against the Federal defenses from the east, west, and south. Fighting furiously, the Confederates drove the Yankees out of Chancellorsville by 10 o'clock that morning, and the Federals retreated north to the Rappahannock. On May 6, 1863, the Army of the Potomac recrossed the river. Once again it had been defeated by Lee's Army of Northern Virginia.

By making a stand at Chancellorsville instead of retreating south, General Lee enabled the Army of Northern Virginia to embark on its second Northern invasion, the Gettysburg campaign, but at a heavy price. Lee lost almost 13,000 men at Chancellorsville, more than 20 percent of his army. Among the dead was his greatest general, Stonewall Jackson. While scouting possible routes of attack on the evening of May 2, Jackson was accidentally shot by his own men on a dark roadway. He died at a field hospital in Guinea Station, Virginia, on May 10, 1863; the building in which he died is preserved as part of the Chancellorsville National Battlefield.

GETTYSBURG

In the wake of Gen. Robert E. Lee's brilliant victory at the Battle of Chancellorsville, the time seemed right for another Confederate invasion of the North. The Union's Army of the Potomac was demoralized, and Lee had an excellent opportunity to move the war in the east out of Virginia and into enemy territory in Pennsylvania. There, Lee could capture badly needed food and supplies for his army and, at the same time, expose the North to the kind of devastation that had proven so costly to the South. Moreover, if he could draw the Army of the Potomac into combat and win another of his strategic victories, he could force an end to the war in the east and possibly secure independence for the Confederacy.

The 73,000 soldiers of the Army of Northern Virginia started their trek northward from Fredericksburg, Virginia, on June 3, 1863. The Confederate forces once again included Lt. Gen. James C. Longstreet's troops, which were reunited with Lee's command after a mission to the south that kept them out of the Battle of Chancellorsville. Lee's forces arrived in southern Pennsylvania around June 24, and they commenced raiding farms and stores throughout the countryside.

As the rebels were making their way northward into Pennsylvania, they were slowly being trailed by the Union troops of the Army of the Potomac. While en route, that army received yet another new commander. President Lincoln had lost confidence in "Fighting Joe" Hooker after Chancellorsville and, on June 28, 1863, he named as his successor Maj. Gen. George Gordon Meade, whose fighting abilities had been proven at the Battle of Fredericksburg.

Meade stepped up the northward march of his 110,000-man army in order to seek out the Confederates in

(Previous page) *A chilly winter dawn rises on the Union artillery positions at Cemetery Ridge near Culp's Hill.*

*The statue of Maj. Gen. Gouverneur K. Warren on Little Round Top. Warren was responsible for getting Union troops to that key position in time to repulse Longstreet's attacking Confederates.*

*Maj. Gen. George Gordon Meade, the newly appointed Federal commander at Gettysburg. (Library of Congress)*

*A monument to the 17th Pennsylvania Cavalry, one of the first units to meet the advancing Confederates on the morning of July 1.*

Pennsylvania. On June 30, one of Meade's lead cavalry units under Maj. Gen. John Buford entered the crossroads village of Gettysburg, Pennsylvania, 8 miles north of the Maryland border. The local residents reported seeing rebel soldiers to the west of town, and Buford posted some troops on a high ground there called Herr Ridge to keep an eye out for the Southerners. Herr Ridge is the westernmost of three ridges which run north–south outside of Gettysburg; the others—major landmarks in the battlefield—are McPherson's Ridge, in the center, and Seminary Ridge (so named for a nearby Lutheran Seminary), which is the closest to the town. Early on the morning of July 1, a group of Confederate soldiers marched eastward into Gettysburg to capture a supply of badly needed shoes. They encountered Buford's cavalrymen at Herr Ridge, a few shots were fired, and the biggest battle ever fought in the Western Hemisphere had begun.

Buford quickly formed his cavalry troopers into a defensive line on McPherson's Ridge northwest of Gettysburg. They held off the Confederates—part of Lt. Gen. Ambrose P. Hill's command—until Union infantry and artillery could be rushed in from the Army of the Potomac's line of march. The first Federal foot soldiers, part of Brig. Gen. John F. Reynolds's command, arrived on the field around 10 a.m. and relieved Buford's men on McPherson's Ridge. They were soon followed by Maj. Gen. Oliver O. Howard's command, which was posted on a defensive line north of town (known today as Howard Lane on the battlefield tour).

The Federal forces in Gettysburg were quickly outnumbered by Confederate reinforcements pouring in from A. P. Hill's corps on the west and Lt. Gen. Richard S. Ewell's corps on the north. Nevertheless, Reynolds's Union soldiers were able to hold their own against Hill's rebels in heavy fighting. By 3 p.m., however, Howard's men could no longer fend off those of Ewell. Many of the Yankees broke ranks and ran away as they had at Chancellorsville, and consequently

*This was the scene that greeted Lt. Gen. James C. Longstreet's Confederate assault troops on the afternoon of July 2, 1863, as they fought their way past Devil's Den, the slope of Little Round Top.*

(Opposite) *Evening on Cemetery Hill, which was held for three bloody days and nights by the Union troops of Maj. Gen. Oliver O. Howard, whose statue overlooks this scene.*

*This detail depicts one of the 110 Union artillery batteries commemorated at Gettysburg—Rickett's Pennsylvanians, on East Cemetery Hill.*

*Artillerymen load their field piece in this close-up of the monument to the New York Light Infantry. They are, left, swabbing out the piece; center, holding a thumb over the fuse vent; and, right, removing a charge from the gunner's haversack.*

*Devil's Den, scene of some of the heaviest fighting on the second day of the battle. Snipers from both North and South made deadly use of these rock formations.*

the Union line north of town collapsed. With Howard's troops in retreat, Ewell's rebels had clear access to the rear of the Federal line on McPherson's Ridge, forcing the Yankees from that position and ending the day's fighting. The Federals retreated through the streets of Gettysburg to a fallback position which General Howard had established a mile south of the town at Cemetery Hill, the site of Gettysburg's Evergreen Cemetery. There, the rest of the Army of the Potomac began gathering on the night of July 1, 1863, while the soldiers of the Army of Northern Virginia continued marching in, north of town.

By daylight on July 2, most of the Union forces had arrived at Gettysburg, as had the Federal commander, General Meade. He posted some of his men east of Cemetery Hill on another rise called Culp's Hill, and the rest on Cemetery Ridge, the high ground running from Cemetery Hill 2½ miles south to a hill called Little Round Top (all major sites today in Gettysburg National Battlefield Park). Lee, facing Meade, was forced to deploy his 50,000 soldiers in a thin line around the Union defenses. He posted Ewell's troops north of Cemetery and Culp's Hills and placed A.P. Hill's men on Seminary Ridge.

On the morning of July 2, Lee opted for a two-pronged assault on the Union lines. He detailed Ewell's corps to move against the Union Army's north end at Culp's Hill while Longstreet's corps, which had just arrived at Gettysburg, attacked the Army of the Potomac's south flank at Little Round Top. Longstreet did not feel the attack was wise and took his time organizing it, hoping that Lee would reconsider. It was 4 p.m. by the time he finally marched his men into attack position at the south end of Seminary Ridge a mile west of Little Round Top (near the battlefield tour's Pitzer Woods). When they arrived there the rebels were shocked to find that Maj. Gen. Daniel E. Sickles's Union troops, who had been on Cemetery Ridge that morning, had moved a half mile to the west, blocking the Confederate advance to Little Round Top. Longstreet's rebels attacked Sickles's

(Clockwise from top) *A Confederate soldier from the Virginia Monument, a Federal fighting man, Brig. Gen. Alexander Hays, a bugler from the Virginia Monument, a Federal cavalry trooper, a Pennsylvania Zouave, and (center) a Confederate with pistol from the Virginia Monument.*

A Union cavalryman. His weapons include a saber, a pistol (on belt), and a seven-shot carbine suspended from the broad strap across his chest. These men moved in squads of four; when they fought dismounted, as they did at Gettysburg, three would maneuver on foot while the fourth soldier held their horses safely out of range.

Yankees at what are known today as the Peach Orchard, the Wheat Field, and Devil's Den—a boulder-strewn no-man's-land at the base of Little Round Top. The Confederates pushed back the Federals in vicious fighting and were only prevented from seizing Little Round Top and rolling up the Union defenses on Cemetery Ridge by the arrival of the last units of the Army of the Potomac, which had just marched in from Maryland. With these fresh troops, the Yankees were able to stop Longstreet's assault and hold the Union line on Cemetery Ridge.

Ewell's attack on the north end of the Union line at Culp's Hill was supposed to have taken place at the same time as Longstreet's assault on Little Round Top. However, Ewell's corps did not attack until after 6 p.m., and his offensive was stopped by nightfall. Moreover, the little ground that Ewell's troops gained on the evening of July 2 was lost in a Yankee counterattack the next morning.

Having failed in assaults on the Union's two flanks, Lee decided that he would have to storm the enemy's center, at Cemetery Ridge. He detailed 13,000 troops under Maj. Gen. George E. Pickett and Brig. Gen. James Pettigrew to undertake this attack—the now legendary Pickett's Charge—on July 3. After a massive, two-hour Confederate artillery bombardment of the Federal fortified positions on Cemetery Hill, Pickett and Pettigrew's 10 brigades formed on Seminary Ridge (near the site of the Virginia Memorial on the battlefield today). At 3 p.m., they started their march 1 mile east to Cemetery Hill. (Although this assault has come to be known as Pickett's Charge, the troops did not attack at a run but marched across to the Union line in parade-ground precision.) The

(Previous pages) *Longstreet's corps first attacked Maj. Gen. Daniel E. Sickles's Union troops on July 2 here at the Peach Orchard.*

The impressive Pennsylvania Monument on Cemetery Ridge. Appropriately the Keystone State had more troops than any other Union state in this battle on its own turf.

General Meade's staff officers following the battle. All of these men played important roles in coordinating the Union defense at Gettysburg. (Library of Congress)

(Opposite) *Maj. Gen. Winfield Scott Hancock, whose Federal troops repelled Pickett's Charge on the third day of the battle. The statue is on East Cemetery Hill.*

*Sunset at the Peach Orchard, looking toward Seminary Ridge, the scene of the first fighting on July 2.*

Southerners deployed toward their objective, a small stand of chestnut oaks near the center of the Union line—the battlefield park's "Copse of Trees"—but they were mowed down at point-blank range by intense Federal artillery and rifle fire. Only a courageous remnant of Confederates made it to the Copse, but they were soon driven back with heavy losses by a fierce Federal counterattack. Repulsed similarly everywhere else, the remainder of the assault forces retreated to Seminary Ridge leaving 7000 dead and wounded strewn on the battlefield behind them.

Lee now realized that he had expected the impossible of these brave assault troops and that the well-entrenched Union defenses could not be broken. On July 4, under the cover of a rainstorm, he led his Army of Northern Virginia southward.

The Battle of Gettysburg represented the high-water mark of the Confederacy. Never before had Lee's army suffered defeat; never again would it be victorious. While Lee inflicted 27,000 casualties on the Union army at Gettysburg, he lost 25,000 men, one-third of his total command. The South simply did not have the manpower to replace these losses; the North did, and this difference would finally spell defeat for the Confederacy.

VICKSBURG

*Ulysses S. Grant, whose success at Vicksburg paved the way for his eventual promotion to Union general-in-chief. (Library of Congress)*

(Previous page) *The war clouds which settled over Vicksburg would decide the fate of the Mississippi Valley.*

Early in the war, President Abraham Lincoln and his military advisors recognized the strategic importance of the Mississippi River, for, if the North could gain control of its waters, the Confederacy would be divided and much easier to defeat. In the first months of 1862, the Union Navy and Army started securing the Mississippi southward from Illinois and northward from the Gulf of Mexico. By October, the entire river lay in Northern hands except for a 130-mile stretch between Port Hudson and Vicksburg, Mississippi.

Vicksburg became the South's last hope for maintaining a hold on the river. The city sat on 200-foot-high bluffs commanding a sharp bend in the Mississippi, and Confederate artillery batteries there kept the river closed to Federal shipping. Vicksburg was protected on the landward side to the east by heavy defenses, and miles of marshlands made attack from the south almost impossible. The city seemed impregnable, and yet the Union had somehow to conquer it if its hold over the rest of the Mississippi were to have the desired effect, that of splitting the Confederacy in two.

The problem of capturing Vicksburg fell to Maj. Gen. U. S. Grant. The "Hero of Fort Donelson" was named commander of the Union forces in the western theater on October 25, 1862, and securing the Mississippi was his first concern. Grant devised a battle plan for taking Vicksburg that called for him to move his army down the western bank of the river and cross eastward at a point well south of the city. From there the Federal forces would march inland and attack the Confederate stronghold from the east, avoiding the Mississippi marshlands to the south.

In January 1863, the Union commander began his Vicksburg campaign. His 35,000-man army left Memphis, Tennessee, crossed over the Mississippi River and started their southerly march down its west bank. After a two-month delay due to winter flooding, they resumed their march. A month later, on April 30,

*A cavalryman from the Wisconsin Monument. At the time, cavalry troopers often dismounted to their rifles.*

Union artillery pieces such as the one shown here were used to shell Vicksburg during the siege. Artillery units were usually organized in batteries of six guns, each with a crew of nine men. The artillerymen had specific duties which included carrying and loading the charges, ramming them down the tube, priming the charge, aiming the piece, firing it, and swabbing down the barrel after each shot.

*The goddess of liberty on Vicksburg's Michigan Monument, located near the site of Michigan's artillery batteries on the siege line.*

116

they recrossed the Mississippi River to Bruinsburg, Mississippi, 30 miles south of Vicksburg.

From Bruinsburg, Grant led his army to Jackson, the Mississippi capital and a vital railroad junction, 60 miles to the northeast. In order to move quickly and ease his supply problems, Grant boldly advanced through this enemy territory, ordering that any food his men could not carry be gathered from the countryside. Rebel troops attempted to halt the Yankee advance in battles at Port Gibson on May 1 and Raymond on May 12, but the Federals easily pushed back the attacking Confederates. Two days later, they marched into Jackson without resistance. From there they moved toward Vicksburg, 40 miles to the west. Repelling further attempts to halt their advance—at Champion Hill, 20 miles east of Vicksburg, and at Big Black River Bridge—the Yankees finally arrived at their destination on May 19.

The line of defensive earthworks facing the Federal troops at Vicksburg extended for almost 7 miles around the city. They began at Fort Hill, a stronghold overlooking the Mississippi River three-quarters of a mile north of the streets of Vicksburg, ran east for a mile and a half to the "Stockade Redan"—a V-shaped stockade fortification—and then curved southward 5 miles to South Fort, which anchored the defenses on the Mississippi below the city. (The northern half of these lines, plus the South Fort site, constitute the current-day Vicksburg National Military Park.) The fortifications were set on high ridges around Vicksburg, and their outer approaches were steep and bordered with hewn trees and other obstacles. Within, the Confederates were prepared with extensive artillery emplacements and trenches for riflemen manned by 23,000 soldiers under the command of Lt. Gen. John C. Pemberton.

Despite the formidable appearance of Vicksburg's defenses, Grant opted for a direct assault on the Confederate works. The Northern troops were a little cocky after their easy victories on the march to the rear of Vicksburg and thought they would be able to capture the town with little opposition. Within hours of the Union arrival on May 19, Maj. Gen. William T. Sherman's soldiers had charged the northeast corner of the rebel defenses (at the battlefield park's Stockade Redan site). Sherman's men were repulsed with heavy losses, and the Federals discovered that winning Vicksburg was not going to be as easy as they had thought.

*Union Brig. Gen. Isaac F. Quinby, a University of Rochester professor who led his forces at Champion's Hill and Vicksburg despite a severe bout with malaria.*

*Brig. Gen. Cadwallader C. Washburn, a Union cavalry commander from Wisconsin who led reinforcements to Grant at Vicksburg. After the war he made a fortune as head of the corporation that would become General Mills.*

*Maj. Gen. Ulysses S. Grant.*

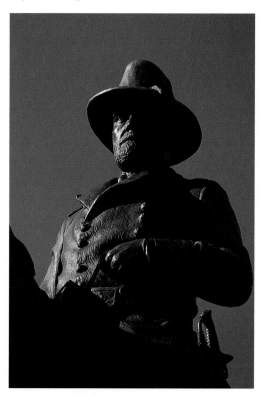

Grant tried one more attack on May 22, a coordinated assault by all 32,000 Union troops against the northern half of the Confederate line. At 10 a.m. Sherman's men attacked the Stockade Redan again while Maj. Gen. James B. McPherson's units moved against the city's Jackson Road approach a half mile to the south. Simultaneously, Maj. Gen. John A. McClernand's forces pressed the rebel defenses near the line of the Southern Railroad 3 miles south of Jackson Road. None of these Federal attacks was successful. For the second time, Sherman's troops were stopped cold at the

*America's Civil War battlefields include some of the nation's most impressive public sculptures. Seen here is the Missouri Monument at Vicksburg.*

*The Old Jackson Road was the approach to Vicksburg guarded by the Great Redoubt and Third Louisiana Redan. It was the scene of heavy fighting by McPherson's Yankees on May 22, 1863.*

Stockade Redan. McPherson's men were thrown back from their assault at Jackson Road, which was guarded by the Third Louisiana Regiment's redan and the "Great Redoubt"* (both of which are significant stops on the Vicksburg battlefield tour). McClernand's troops initially fared better in their attack to the south, breaking through the Confederate defenses at the Railroad Redoubt and the Second Texas Regiment lunette.† But without reinforcements, they could not maintain their hold within the rebel lines and, at around 5:30 p.m., they were forced out of their newly won positions by a Confederate counterattack.

Having twice failed to take Vicksburg by storm, General Grant realized that the Union army would have to lay siege to the town, sealing it off from the outside world until its defenses

*A redan is a V-shaped fortification; a redoubt is a multisided fortification, usually with artillery emplacements.
†A crescent-shaped earthwork.

(Opposite) *This statue honors Capt. Andrew Hickenlooper, McPherson's Chief Engineer, who supervised construction of the Union trenches and developed the plan to tunnel beneath the Confederate defenses.*

*One of the Union batteries that pounded the defenses of Vicksburg during Grant's 47-day siege.*

could be breached or its defenders starved into submission. Grant immediately sent north for reinforcements. By June 18, he had 77,000 soldiers spread over a 12-mile line enclosing Vicksburg from the landward side. U.S. Navy gunboats had sneaked past the city's artillery. Now the Mississippi River was blockaded north and south of Vicksburg, and the city's inhabitants—soldiers and civilians alike—were cut off from any supplies and reinforcements.

Once Vicksburg was sealed off, the Yankees commenced an unceasing bombardment that soon forced city residents to live in "bombproofs"— underground shelters—as well as cope with ever-diminishing supplies of food, water, and medicine. Grant also had his troops dig trenches toward the Vicksburg defenses, cut in

a zigzag pattern to avoid Confederate rifle fire; in some places, these trenches came within 15 feet of the rebel lines (those dug by Brig. Gen. Alvin P. Hovey's troops may be viewed at the Hovey's Approach site on the battlefield).

In addition to digging trenches, the army tunneled under the Confederate defenses and attempted to blow them up. Indeed, two large mines were ignited under the Third Louisiana Regiment's redan near Jackson Road on June 25 and July 1. The explosions failed to breach the rebel defense but they helped convince the Confederate commander, General Pemberton, that he could not hold Vicksburg for much longer.

At 3 p.m. on July 3, Pemberton met with Grant to discuss terms. The place, east of the Confederate's Great Redoubt, has been preserved as the

"Surrender Interview Site." Grant wanted an unconditional surrender, but Pemberton, seeking to shield his troops from prisoner-of-war camps, insisted that his men be paroled (released on their word not to fight again until exchanged for similarly paroled Northerners). Grant accepted Pemberton's condition in return for the Confederates' surrender on Independence Day, realizing that such a victory on the anniversary of America's birth would be a great morale booster for the Union.

At 10 a.m. on July 4, 1863, the Confederate troops along Vicksburg's defenses laid down their arms and allowed the Union soldiers into their lines. The Yankees, who had developed great respect for the rebels' spirit during the siege, did not jeer their defeated enemies, and Grant ordered food distributed to both soldiers and civilians. On hearing that Vicksburg had fallen the Confederate commander at Port Hudson, Mississippi, also surrendered, and the Mississippi River was won for the Union.

*The Illinois Monument is based on the Roman Pantheon. Illinois had more soldiers at Vicksburg than any other Northern state.*

# CHICKAMAUGA

In the summer of 1863, as Federal armies were winning in Gettysburg and Vicksburg, Union troops were driving the Confederate army out of Tennessee as well. In early September, Maj. Gen. William S. Rosecrans's 57,000 troops captured Chattanooga, and forced the last of the state's rebel forces—an army of 30,000 under Gen. Braxton Bragg—to retreat 26 miles south to the mountains near LaFayette, Georgia.

Rosecrans pursued Bragg, dividing the Union army to better seek out the

(Previous page) *The Florida Monument, located at the northern end of the battlefield near Battle Line Drive.*

*Statuary on the Michigan Monument depicts a rifleman engaged in the sniping which characterized much of the Battle of Chickamauga.*

hiding rebels. Unknown to the Union commander, however, Bragg had been receiving heavy reinforcements at LaFayette. Troops from throughout the Confederacy, including those of Lt. Gen. James C. Longstreet (from Gen. Robert E. Lee's Army of Northern Virginia) were being sent to aid in the recapture of Chattanooga. Thus, while Rosecrans thought he was pursuing an enemy of 30,000 men, he was actually facing more than 70,000, who were waiting to trap his divided forces.

Rosencrans became aware of the Confederate buildup on September 12 and quickly tried to reunite his outnumbered command, ordering his units to gather at Lee & Gordon's gristmill on the west bank of Chickamauga Creek, about 10 miles south of Chattanooga. Bragg inexplicably did not attempt to intercept the Yankees

as they regrouped, and by September 17 all of Rosecrans's troops had assembled at the designated rendezvous.

With the Union army in place, Bragg decided to march his forces northward around the Federal position and cut off Rosecrans's army from Chattanooga. He helped to recapture the city and isolate the Yankees so that they could be attacked at will.

General Bragg started his northward movement on the morning of September 18, marching his troops east of Chickamauga Creek and a few miles northeast of Lee & Gordon's gristmill. By noon he shifted to the west to complete his encirclement of the Union army. He planned on crossing the Chickamauga at Dalton's Ford, Thedford Ford, and Alexander Bridge (the

The fighting at Snodgrass Hill may well have been like this reenacted scene at New Market. Such reenactments help make these 125-year-old events come alive for thousands of participants and spectators throughout the United States each year.

southeast corner of today's Chickamauga Battlefield Park) and at Reed's Bridge 3 miles to the northeast, but when he arrived at these crossings he found them guarded by Federal cavalry. (Rosecrans had spotted Bragg's troop movements that morning and sent some cavalry units northward to hold off the Southerners until the Yankee infantry could be put into a defensive alignment.) The Union cavalry prevented much of Bragg's army from crossing the Chickamauga until after 4 p.m., thus allowing Rosecrans ample time to deploy his riflemen along defensive positions facing the enemy.

By the morning of September 19, the Federal lines extended 4 miles north from Lee & Gordon's mill to the Kelly House. Bragg's Confederates were spread about a half mile to the east of the Yankee lines. Surrounding the armies was a dense forest that made reconnaissance and communication extremely difficult. Indeed, the terrain would have a deciding effect on the battle to follow.

*Most of the fighting at Chickamauga took place in the dense woods seen on the horizon, rather than on the open field seen in the foreground.*

The battlefield's Dyer Cabin recreates a Union-held structure that the Confederates secured during the fighting. The flag is the Confederate battle flag, which was used exclusively by the South's armed forces, not as the national colors.

On the morning of September 19, the commander at the north end of the Union line, Maj. Gen. George H. Thomas, sent a division of his troops eastward toward Chickamauga Creek to push back what he thought was one small rebel unit. When his soldiers reported that there was a substantial force of Southerners in front of them (the entire Confederate army was, in fact, west of the creek), Thomas ordered a general attack. His units moved a mile east of the LaFayette Road (now U.S. Route 27, the major north–south road within the Chickamauga Battlefield Park). There they encountered the Confederate cavalry commanded by Lt. Gen. Nathan B. Forrest and Maj. Gen. William H. T. Walker along what is now called Battle Line Road.

Thomas's assault quickly led to Confederate counterattacks against the entire Union line, and by midday fighting was heavy throughout the battlefield. Around 2:30 p.m., the Confederates under Lt. Gen. Alexander P. Stewart managed to break through the Union center. They drove Brig. Gen. H. P. VanCleve's Yankees back almost a mile and divided the northern and southern halves of the Union army. Stewart's men in turn were driven off under heavy fire from Federal artillery under the command of Eli Lilly—who in later years went on to found the famous pharmaceutical company—and the troops under Col. John T. Wilder who were armed with new, seven-shot Spencer repeating rifles that were vastly superior to the rebels' single-shot weapons.

*Confederate Lt. Gen. John B. Hood, who had a leg amputated following a wound at Chicka- mauga. This courageous field commander had previously lost the use of an arm at Gettys- burg. (Library of Congress).*

*Maj. Gen. George H. Thomas, the ''Rock of Chickamauga,'' who saved the Northern army with his stand on Snodgrass Hill. (Library of Congress)*

*The Brotherton Cabin on the LaFayette Road opposite the Confederate Breakthrough site. Rebel troops swarmed past here on the afternoon of September 20, 1863, routing most of the Union army.*

Wilder's decisive counterattack against Stewart's forces saved the Union army that day; it is commemorated by the battlefield's Wilder Tower observation platform.

Following Stewarts' retreat, Bragg launched an attack against Maj. Gen. Philip H. Sheridan's troops on the south end of the Union line. But it was unsuccessful, and the day's fighting wound down. By nightfall the Union army was firmly in control of the LaFayette Road for 2½ miles north of Lee & Gordon's mill, and for a mile beyond that to the east (along today's Battle Line Drive).

The Confederates resumed their attack on the Union lines the following morning, with Bragg driving hard against Thomas's position on the north and Sheridan's on the south. Still the Federal troops held their own against the rebel offensive until 11 a.m., when Rosecrans made a fatal blunder. The Union commander had received a false report that Brig. Gen. John M. Brannan's unit had pulled back from the center of the Union line on LaFayette Road, leaving a gap. Rosecrans, unable to see Brannan's troops through the dense forest, ordered the next unit to the south—that of Brig. Gen. Thomas J. Wood—to move into Brannan's position. Wood protested that Brannan's troops were in place, but Rosecrans would not change his order. Obeying his superior's direct command, Wood shifted his troops, creating a real opening in the Union line. Seizing upon this opportunity, Longstreet's hard-fighting force burst into the gap. Before the Yankees knew what had hit them, their center and southern flanks had collapsed in a rout. Rosecrans was forced from his headquarters in hasty retreat, and the only commander left on the field was General Thomas to the north.

Thomas quickly formed the retreating Federal units into a defensive line on Snodgrass Hill, just west of his own position (the hill was named for George Snodgrass, whose cabin was on the site). That afternoon, Thomas's troops repulsed numerous Confederate assaults against the hill. They saved the Union army and earned Thomas the sobriquet "Rock of Chickamauga."

At nightfall, the battle came to an end. Rosecrans's army, which had suffered 18,000 casualties, had been defeated by Bragg's Confederates, but it was a costly victory for the South. Bragg's troops had borne 16,000 casualties and had little to show for this loss except the strategically unimportant Chickamauga battlefield. Bragg, a less aggressive fighter than Lee or Longstreet, did not pursue Rosecrans's shattered forces. Believing his troops to be exhausted, he permitted the Yankees to retreat to the safety of Chattanooga, and the South lost its best chance to drive the Union army from Tennessee.

*The desperate artillery fire which held the Federal position on Snodgrass Hill is depicted in this detail of the First Ohio's Monument.*

*This rifleman wears the broad-brimmed slouch hat which the western troops preferred over the standard Union cap (kepi).*

*This monument to the 16th U.S. Infantry captures the fighting that took place in the heavy woods at Chickamauga. Most Northern troops in the war were state volunteers; very few were professional U.S. Army Regulars like the 16th.*

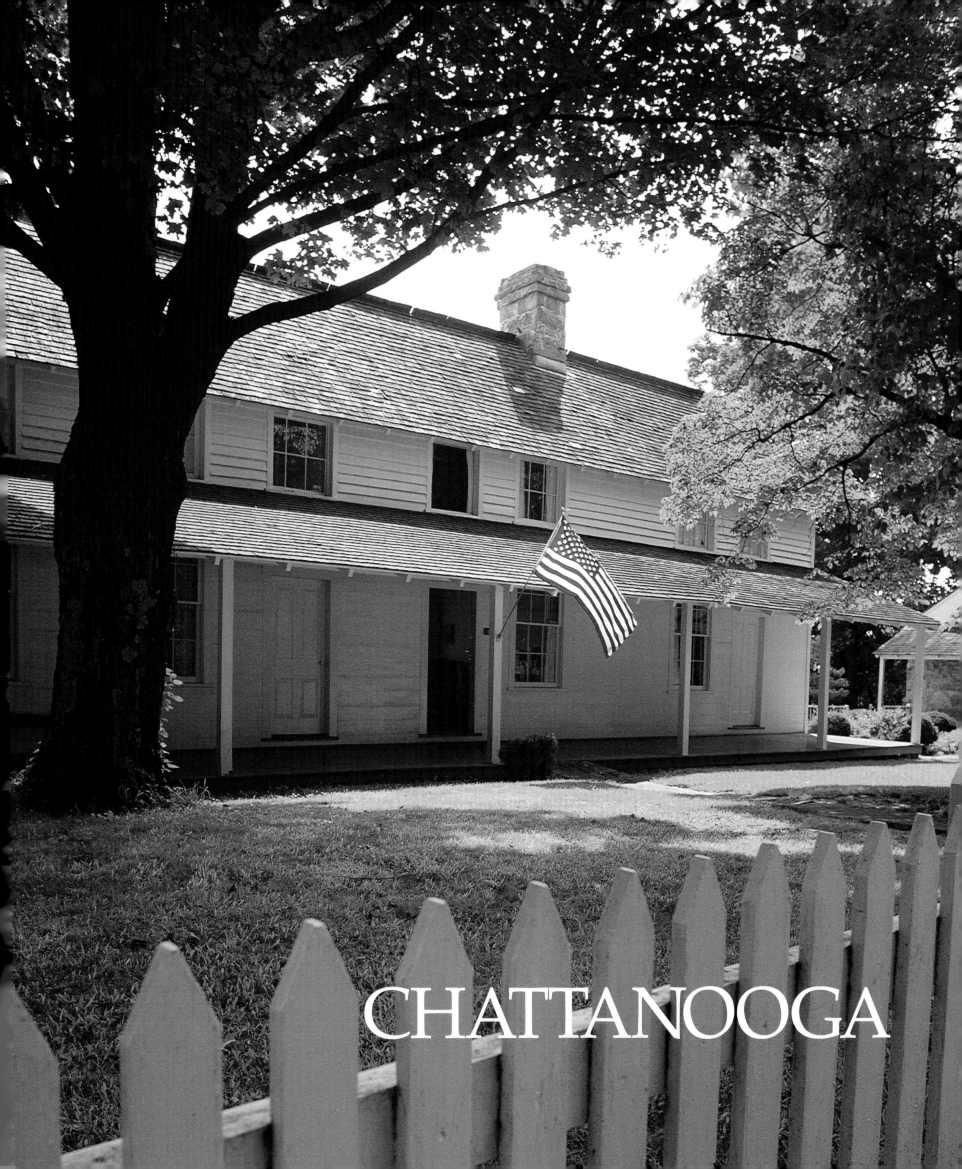

CHATTANOOGA

The sweeping curve of the Tennessee River viewed from Lookout Mountain. Moccasin Point—the aptly named peninsula within the curve—was the area that the Union army's supply line traversed on its route to Chattanooga, to the lower right.

(Previous page) *The Cravens House, a Confederate headquarters on Lookout Mountain, was the scene of the heaviest fighting in the "Battle Above the Clouds."*

Maj. Gen. William S. Rosecrans's Federal army retreated to Chattanooga, Tennessee, following the Union defeat at the Battle of Chickamauga on September 20, 1863. Chattanooga lay on the south side of the Tennessee River, within the upper loop of the waterway's broad S-shaped curve. The Union troops quickly began constructing a series of defensive earthworks enclosing all of Chattanooga on the landward side. By the time Gen. Braxton Bragg's Confederates made their way there from Chickamauga on September 24, Rosecrans's 40,000 Yankees were firmly entrenched in the city. Unable to storm the Federal lines, Bragg was force to mount a siege in order to capture Chattanooga and its defending army.

Bragg deployed his troops along a 5-mile line south of the Yankees' trenches. The Confederates' right was anchored on Missionary Ridge, a steep outcropping (named for an old Spanish mission once located there) that extended for 20 miles south of Chattanooga. The rebel siege line snaked its way from the ridge to a small rise called Orchard Knob and across Chattanooga Valley to Lookout Mountain on the west. The mountain was a rock-crowned precipice overlooking Chattanooga and abutting the south shore of the Tennessee River at the lower loop of its S curve. Bragg quick-

ly placed his artillery on Lookout Mountain and in Lookout Valley beyond it, closing the Tennessee River to Federal shipping from the west and cutting off Rosecrans's main supply line to the U.S. Army depot at Bridgeport, Alabama, 25 miles away. With the river closed and his soldiers enveloping Chattanooga to the south, Bragg planned to slowly starve Rosecrans into surrender in a Confederate version of the siege of Vicksburg.

When the War Department in Washington became advised of Rosecrans's predicament, it quickly ordered Federal reinforcements to Chattanooga. Maj. Gen. William T. Sherman was sent from Mississippi with 17,000 men, and 20,000 troops were dispatched from the Army of the Potomac to serve under Maj. Gen. "Fighting Joe" Hooker. President Lincoln sent one other soldier to see that these reinforcements did their job: Ulysses S. Grant, who was now promoted to commander of all the Union forces in the west, including those in Tennessee and those in the Mississippi Valley. At the same time, Rosecrans was replaced as commander of the forces already in Chattanooga by Maj. Gen. George H. Thomas, who had saved the Union army at Chickamauga.

By the time Grant arrived at Chattanooga on October 23—coming in from the north and crossing the Tennessee River directly into the city, a route

*The 97th Ohio Regiment, according to its marker at the Bragg Reservation, was the first Federal unit to enter Chattanooga in September 1863.*

*The commanding heights of Lookout Mountain overlooking the curving Tennessee River, which can be seen to the right of the cannon barrel.*

which was still open to the Federals—the situation for Thomas's troops had become dire. The men were down to quarter rations, and many had been reduced to eating roasted acorns to survive. Hundreds of army horses and mules had starved to death, and it seemed that Thomas's soldiers would soon share that fate. Grant immediately took steps to get supplies. He ordered Hooker's newly arrived troops to sweep the rebels from Lookout Valley. He then had a pontoon bridge erected across the Tennessee River at the northern end of the valley out of range of the Confederate guns. Supplies could thus be shipped from Bridgeport, Alabama, to the valley, then be carried across the bridge and into the city over the route used by Grant to reach Chattanooga. On October 30 the shipments began, and by the time Sherman's 17,000 soldiers arrived in Chattanooga on November 14, Thomas's beleaguered troops were again well fed and anxious to fight.

Sherman's reinforcements increased the Union army in Chattanooga to more than 77,000 men, and Grant was now ready for a counter offensive against the surrounding Confederates. His first target was Orchard Knob, which was a good stepping-off point for an assault against Missionary Ridge. On November 23, he directed the troops under Maj. Gen. Philip H. Sheridan and Brig. Gen. Thomas J. Wood to assault the position. They quickly stormed the rise—now one of the Chattanooga Battlefield Park's principal sites—and drove its defending Confederates back to Missionary Ridge as planned.

With Orchard Knob secured, Grant next focused his attention on General Hooker's troops in the valley west of Lookout Mountain. To get them east where they would be needed for the assault on Missionary Ridge, he ordered "Fighting Joe" to have his men work their way in small groups directly up the side of Lookout Mountain and to drive the Confederate soldiers from the peak in the process. Hooker began his attack on the morning of November 24, moving up the northwest slope of the mountain (most of which is now part of the Chatta-

*Orchard Knob, with the Illinois Monument in the foreground. Generals Grant and Thomas had their headquarters here during the assault on Missionary Ridge.*

A Union sentinel on guard duty. The boredom of the same routine day after day was one of the worst aspects of sieges like that at Chattanooga.

nooga Battlefield Park). It was a cold, misty morning, and fog shrouded the lower reaches of the peak, hiding Hooker's troops from the rebel artillery above and thus giving the action its name, "the Battle Above the Clouds." The Yankees drove back Bragg's Southerners in heavy fighting around the Cravens House, on the north side of the mountain. By nightfall Hooker's troops had secured the mountain, but the Yankees in the valley below did not know of his victory until the following morning, when the Stars and Stripes were seen flying from the mountain's highest peak. (This summit is now the site of the battlefield park's Adolph Ochs Museum and Overlook, named for the *New York Times* publisher who was largely responsible for the preserva-

tion of Lookout Mountain as a battlefield site.)

With the mountain in Union hands, Grant could finally mount a Federal attack against the Confederate forces on Missionary Ridge. Sherman's troops began the offensive at 11 o'clock on November 25, when they advanced against the northern end of the ridge. They met heavy resistance from the Confederate forces of Maj. Gen. Patrick Cleburne, a hard-fighting Irishman who had immigrated to Arkansas and sided with the South at the beginning of the war. The Yankees made little headway in the face of Cleburne's opposition, and the Federal offensive stalled.

While Sherman was attacking the north end of the ridge, Hooker was supposed to assault the southern flank. However, the Confederates had burned the one bridge over Chatta-

*An artillery position at Sherman Reservation, where Maj. Gen. William T. Sherman's attack on the northern end of Missionary Ridge was stalled. On the right is Lookout Mountain, 7 miles to the southwest.*

*These stone steps assist visitors to the battle-field in walking up Lookout Mountain. Hooker's soldiers had no such help making the difficult climb.*

*Beleaguered Union troops camped near Citico Creek, Chattanooga. Their simple winter quarters consisted of log bases covered with tents. (Library of Congress)*

nooga Creek, which Hooker needed to reach his objective, and his attack was delayed until he could reconstruct the bridge, although some of his units (without artillery) managed to ford the creek by 3 p.m.

With Sherman stopped on the north and Hooker not even in place on the south, the Union assault on Missionary Ridge was foundering. To divert the Confederate pressure on Sherman, Grant ordered Thomas's troops on Orchard Knob to attack the trenches at the base of Missionary Ridge at 3 p.m. Sheridan and Wood's units had been waiting to get into action all day and sprang at the chance. They quickly swarmed into the entrenchments and then, without waiting for further orders, continued their assault up Missionary's 400-foot face. Grant was dumbfounded, believing that the center of the Confederate line was too strong for his forces to penetrate. He ordered a halt to the advance, but the attacking troops, seeing the enemy wavering, would not be stopped. They pushed Bragg's rebels from the crest of Missionary Ridge (along the battlefield park's Crest Road), capturing thousands of prisoners and driving the rest of the Southerners down the eastern slopes of the ridge in a rout. With the Confederate center overrun, Bragg's troops to the north and south were forced to withdraw, and Grant's Yankees had won back Chattanooga.

The Union victory at Chattanooga had far-reaching effects. The Confederacy had lost Tennessee, and the United States had gained a stepping-off point for a decisive campaign through Georgia—the "March to the Sea" which General Sherman would mount the following year. Perhaps most importantly, the victory led directly to Grant's promotion to general-in-chief of the entire U.S. Army. President Lincoln had finally found the commander who would lead the Union forces to victory.

*The rocky face of Lookout Mountain, scene of the ''Battle Above the Clouds.''*

*An artilleryman—identified by the rammer in his right hand—part of the Bragg Reservation Monument on Missionary Ridge.*

# KENNESAW MOUNTAIN

Confederate Gen. Joseph E. Johnston, who hoped to lure Sherman's army into a decisive battle at Kennesaw Mountain. (Library of Congress)

Maj. Gen. William Tecumseh Sherman, the Union commander who declared that ''War is hell''—and proceeded to prove it. Sherman recognized that, in order to win, the Union had to destroy the Confederacy's will to fight as well as its armies. (Library of Congress)

(Previous page) This photo shows the commanding view enjoyed by Gen. Joseph E. Johnston's Confederates atop Kennesaw Mountain as they awaited Maj. Gen. William T. Sherman's Union army to the north.

After the Confederate defeat at Chattanooga, Tennessee, in November 1863, Gen. Braxton Bragg's forces retreated 25 miles southeast to Dalton, Georgia. There, they gathered behind the safety of Rocky Face Ridge, a massive stone outcrop, to regroup and count their losses. Their army, which had stood at just 40,000 men before the battle, had sustained heavy casualties; as many as 6500 soldiers had been killed or captured on Missionary Ridge alone. Worse still, the men had lost all faith in their commander, blaming Bragg for their loss to the army that they had defeated at Chickamauga. Indeed, morale among the troops was so low that a high desertion rate further weakened the army's depleted ranks.

Confederate President Jefferson Davis, a personal friend of Bragg, had supported the general as long as he could, but was finally forced to remove him from command in late December. His replacement was Gen. Joseph E. Johnston, who had previously commanded the Confederate army during the Peninsular campaign. Johnston quickly took steps to improve conditions in his new command. He allowed his soldiers to go on furlough—something Bragg never did—and declared amnesty for deserters who returned. He also arranged for badly needed food and fresh uniforms. Within weeks the morale of Johnston's troops improved, deserters started coming back, and new recruits began swelling the Southerners' ranks. By April 1864, Johnston's army had grown to 45,000 men and was once again ready to fight.

While the Confederates were recouping at Rocky Face Ridge, the Federal forces in Chattanooga were preparing for a new Southern offensive. Their ranks now stood at more than 100,000 men under Maj. Gen. William Tecumseh Sherman, who took command of the western army

(Opposite page) Artillery batteries such as these dueled back and forth on General Sherman's first days at Kennesaw. Unable to dislodge Johnston's troops with cannonfire, the Union commander opted for a direct attack on the mountain's heights.

after Ulysses S. Grant's elevation to Federal general-in-chief in March 1864. As part of Grant's "offensive on all fronts" plan, Sherman was ordered to lead his troops across Georgia, splitting apart the southeastern Confederacy.

Sherman started his march south from Chattanooga on May 4, heading toward Johnston's position at Rocky Face Ridge. The Union commander's strategy was to hold the Confederates at Rocky Face with a portion of his forces while the rest of the Federal army circled to the southeast to surround Johnston and cut his access to the Western & Atlantic Railroad and thereby sever his supply line to Atlanta. Johnston moved south ahead of the Yankees, however, marching his army 12 miles down the railroad line to Resaca, Georgia. There, he was reinforced by 15,000 Alabamans serving under Lt. Gen. Leonidas Polk. Sherman's troops caught up with the Confederates at Resaca on May 13 but, after two days of indecisive fighting, both armies pulled back.

In the month following the Battle of Resaca, Sherman made several attempts to get around Johnston's army and cut the Confederates' rail link with Atlanta, but Johnston kept slipping away southward along the railroad ahead of him, happy to be drawing the Federal army farther from its base of operations in Chattanooga and closer to the Confederate base in Atlanta. Ultimately Johnston hoped he could maneuver the Yankees into combat on terrain of his choosing, where his badly outnumbered Confederates could deal the enemy a crippling blow.

On June 19, the two armies stopped to confront each other near Marietta, Georgia, 50 miles south of Resaca and just 15 miles northwest of Atlanta. Johnston arrived first and deployed his troops around Kennesaw Mountain, a natural defensive position northwest of the town, where they dug in on a 6-mile line centered on the mountain (today their trenches remain a major feature of the battlefield park). Assigned to hold Kennesaw Mountain were Polk's corps, under

Union soldiers in the field wearing lightweight campaign dress, with their trouser legs tucked into their heavy wool socks. The private on the right wears the slouch hat preferred by Sherman's western troops. Behind them are the "dog tents" carried on the march, forerunners of World War II's pup tents.

*This cabin—the Valentine Kolb farmhouse at the southwestern end of the battlefield—is the only wartime building extant at Kennesaw Mountain.*

the leadership of Maj. Gen. William W. Loring, who assumed command after General Polk's death in action on June 14. Lt. Gen. John B. Hood's troops were placed to Loring's right, facing north; Lt. Gen. William J. Hardee's command was positioned to Loring's left, facing west.

By the time Sherman's forces arrived at Kennesaw Mountain late on June 19, the Confederates were firmly entrenched. Sherman attempted to dislodge the Southerners with heavy artillery barrages, but to no avail; the Confederates merely returned the fire from their positions on Kennesaw and inflicted as much damage as they received. The Union commander then returned to his strategy of trying to outflank Johnston by sending Maj.

Gen. John M. Schofield's troops around to the southeast to turn the rebel's southern flank held by Hardee about 4 miles south of the mountain. Johnston noticed the Yankee troop movement and quickly countered by shifting Hood's forces from the right end of the Confederate defenses to the left. Hood's troops assumed their new position near the Valentine Kolb farmhouse (a major site on the battlefield tour today). On June 22, Hood attacked Schofield's approaching Yankees, but the rebels were repulsed with heavy casualties. Unable to force Schofield back, they returned to their trenches near the Kolb farmhouse.

Federal troops sustained heavy casualties while moving up Kennesaw's steep, rocky slopes, such as this portion of Pigeon Hill.

Johnston's Confederates held back the advancing Yankees from breastworks such as these.

Following this Federal victory, Sherman decided to try a direct assault against the entire Confederate army. The Southerners' ranks were thinly stretched around Kennesaw, and the Union commander felt that his troops could probably break through Johnston's lines despite the rebels' excellent defensive positions. On June 27, Sherman launched a three-pronged attack. Maj. Gen. James B. McPherson's troops were to move against Loring's force on the southern end of Kennesaw Mountain, while Maj. Gen. George H. Thomas's Yankees assaulted Hardee's men farther south at Cheatham's Hill and Schofield renewed his attack against Hood.

McPherson's troops started their advance, pushing their way past the Confederate trenches at the foot of Kennesaw Mountain. But their march to the summit stalled under heavy rifle fire from the crest. When the rebels began rolling boulders down the mountainside, McPherson was forced to order a retreat.

Thomas was doing no better in his assault at Cheatham's Hill, where his troops, advancing against the hill's northern face, were cut down by a withering rebel crossfire likened by one survivor to a severe hailstorm. Thomas's soldiers were driven back with heavy losses, and the area of their attack, now a major battlefield site, became known as Kennesaw's "Dead Angle."

Like McPherson and Thomas, Schofield was also unable to dislodge Hood's defensive position. However, he was able to fight his way around Hood's southern flank, threatening to get between the Confederate army and Atlanta. This maneuver proved the battle's decisive moment, for Johnston, faced with the prospect of being cut off from the Confederate headquarters, was forced to leave Kennesaw Mountain and resume his march southward toward Atlanta on July 2.

Kennesaw Mountain offered General Johnston his best opportunity to lure Sherman into a battle that could have crippled the Union army in Georgia,

HARKER'S ATTACK

Brig. Gen. Charles G. Harker rode into the battle mounted on a white horse while leading a column of eight Union regiments. In previous battles, Harker had four horses killed under him but he escaped injury. Intense Confederate fire broke the Union attack and the survivors fled to a ravine about 100 yards to your front. General Harker, a conspicuous target while rallying his troops, was shot from his horse mortally wounded. No further attacks took place at this location.

*This marker shows the area from which Brig. Gen. Charles G. Harker led an unsuccessful assault against Cheatham Hill on June 27, 1863. Badly wounded here, Harker died a few hours later.*

*The Illinois Memorial on Cheatham Hill, scene of some of the fiercest fighting at Kennesaw Mountain. Nearby was the fateful Dead Angle where Maj. Gen. George H. Thomas's Yankees were mowed down by heavy fire.*

but Sherman was too good a field commander to be drawn into such a trap. While Sherman made an attempt to storm the Confederate position near Marietta, he did not press the attack when it became apparent his forces could not succeed. As a result, he lost only 3500 of his 100,000 troops, hardly the crushing blow that Johnston needed to even the odds between the two armies. Subsequently, the Confederates were forced south into Atlanta (now under General Hood, who had replaced Johnston on July 17 by order of Jefferson Davis). Sherman followed closely behind. After a series of battles, Atlanta fell on September 1. From there, Sherman began his "March to the Sea" in November 1864, ruthlessly laying waste to a broad swath of the Georgia countryside and destroying Confederate morale in the process.

*Sumac on Pigeon Hill.*

# THE WILDERNESS
# & SPOTSYLVANIA

*The rolling countryside where Grant and Lee's soldiers struggled for supremacy at Spotsylvania. Like many Civil War battle sites, Spotsylvania was not in itself of strategic importance, but a place where two armies happened to meet.*

*(Previous page) The Federal fighting man is depicted on the 15th New Jersey Regiment Monument at Spotsylvania's Bloody Angle.*

In March 1864, Ulysses S. Grant was summoned to Washington, D.C., to take charge of the entire Union Army. His victories at Shiloh, Vicksburg, and Chattanooga had convinced President Lincoln that he was the best field commander the United States had, and Lincoln designated him for promotion to the revived permanent rank of lieutenant general—a three-star grade that had previously been held only by George Washington. Congress promptly authorized the promotion.

As lieutenant general, Grant outranked every other Federal commander, giving the former Illinois storekeeper the power to coordinate the campaigns of all of the U.S. troops in the war. Grant quickly took advantage of this position, realizing that the piecemeal Federal offensives waged to that point had permitted the Confederates to move troops from front to front wherever they were needed most. To counter this, Grant ordered a series of simultaneous Union offensives in May 1864 against the rebel forces in Georgia, eastern Virginia, and the Shenandoah Valley in order to pressure the overtaxed defenses of the Confederacy until they broke.

Grant himself assumed control of the Federal assault against Robert E. Lee's Army of Northern Virginia, attaching himself to the Army of the Potomac, which continued to be commanded by Maj. Gen. George Gordon Meade but which was under Grant's overall direction. At that time Meade's army was still in its winter camp near Culpeper, Virginia, north of the Rapidan River. Lee's army was encamped on the other side of the Rapidan at Orange, Virginia, about 15 miles to the southwest. Grant decided to move his army of 100,000 men to the southeast, across the Rapidan. There, he would attempt to edge between the rebel forces at Orange and the Confederate capital of Richmond, luring Lee's 60,000 Confederates into open combat.

The Army of the Potomac crossed the Rapidan on May 4, moving south into the Wilderness—the area of dense forest and underbrush west of

BATTLE OF THE WILDERNESS
HERE MAY 5.6.1864. 70,000 CONFEDERATES UNDER
LEE DEFEATED 120,000 FEDERALS UNDER GRANT.
CONFEDERATE LOSS 11,500. FEDERAL 18,000.
THIS BATTLE, FOUGHT WITH CONSPICUOUS BRAVERY.
IN A WILDERNESS ON FIRE, WILL TAKE IT'S PLACE
AMONG THE GREAT BATTLES OF THE CIVIL WAR
ERECTED BY THE 13. VIRGINIA REGIMENT. CHAPTER. U.D.C.
• 1927 •

*''This battle, fought with conspicuous bravery in a wilderness on fire, will take its place among the great battles of the Civil War''—so predicts this plaque, which was dedicated by the United Daughters of the Confederacy in 1927. The opinion has stood the test of time.*

151

A federal bugler (left) and drummers. The army used drum, fife, and bugle calls to regulate camp activities and give orders during battles; in densely wooded areas like the Wilderness, this was the only way to transmit instructions quickly. Musicians on both sides were often young boys who could not yet shoulder a musket.

Chancellorsville where "Fighting Joe" Hooker had been trapped a year earlier. In their path lay Wildnerness Tavern, which can be seen today at the northeast corner of the Wilderness Battlefield Park. The tavern's foundations stood at the intersection of the Germanna Plank Road and the Orange Turnpike. The latter ran east–west from Orange to Fredericksburg. South of the tavern, another route, Brock Road, ran southeasterly from the Orange Turnpike to the village of Spotsylvania Court House, 11 miles away.

Lee became aware of the Union troop movements around Wilderness Tavern on May 4, and quickly dispatched Lt. Gen. Richard S. Ewell and Lt. Gen. Ambrose P. Hill to stop the Federal advance. (The third corps of Lee's army, that of Lt. Gen. James C. Longstreet, was still on its way to join Lee from its previous assignment in Tennessee.) Ewell's forces marched east from the Confederate camp along the Orange Turnpike; Hill's men went along the Orange Plank Road, which ran a couple of miles south of the Turnpike, gradually curving northward until the two roads merged 3 miles east of Wildnerness Tavern.

The Federals detected the Confederate advance along the Orange Turnpike early on May 5, and Maj. Gen. Gouverneur K. Warren's Yankees were sent to turn back Ewell's forces. Warren supported by Maj. Gen. John Sedgwick's troops, began his offensive around 1 p.m., fighting on both sides of the Turnpike west of the tavern. Shortly thereafter, Maj. Gen. Winfield Scott Hancock was dispatched down Brock Road to hold back Hill's Confederates, who had arrived to the south of Ewell along the Orange Plank Road. Hancock's force engaged the Southerners near what is now called the Brock Road–Plank Road intersection.

The combat between the Yankees and Confederates was described afterward as "bushwhacking on a grand scale." The dense forest of the Wilderness precluded any semblance of order within the armies. Units were

(Opposite page) *The soldiers of both armies became lost in the tangled maze of the Wilderness, where the fighting was described as "bushwhacking on a grand scale."*

*Union Brig. Gen. James S. Wadsworth, who was wounded in the head while leading his men at the Wilderness. He was captured, and subsequently died in a Confederate field hospital on May 8, 1864. (Library of Congress)*

*A memorial to Wadsworth on the battlefield.*

isolated from each other, and the troops often fired blindly on friend and foe alike. Adding to the confusion were the fires that sporadically erupted as the dry underbrush caught the flash of the soldiers' rifles; many wounded men were burned to death where they lay.

When the fighting died down at dusk on May 5, the Confederates dug in between the Turnpike and Plank Road (along the battlefield park's Hill–Ewell Drive, where many of the rebel trenches have been preserved). The Federals remained facing them with Sedgwick's troops north of the Turnpike, Warren's men to the south, and Hancock's soldiers straddling the Orange Plank Road west of Brock Road.

*The dense forest and underbrush which gave the Wilderness its name is seen here from the Confederate trenches dug along the battlefield's Hill–Ewell Drive after the first day's fighting.*

The fighting resumed at dawn on May 6, when Grant's Yankees mounted a heavy assault against Hill's troops on the Plank Road and drove them back almost a mile to Lee's headquarters at Tapp Farm. Just as Hill's line was crumbling, Longstreet's troops reached Orange Plank Road. They immediately launched a counter attack that almost drove the Northerners back a mile and a quarter, saving Lee and the remainder of Hill's command. Then they attacked the Union's southern flank, rolling up Hancock's line and scattering the Yankees. Lee followed this with an attack on Sedgwick's troops north of the Turnpike, and by nightfall on May 6 the Union army had been badly battered.

Grant had lost almost 18,000 men in two day's fighting and had gained nothing in return. But instead of retreating in the face of these losses, as the Army of the Potomac had always done before, he opted to force Lee into open combat outside of the Wilderness. On May 7, he marched his troops south, down Brock Road toward Spotsylvania Court House in an effort to get between the Confederate army and Richmond. Once Lee realized Grant's objective, he rushed his troops southward to get to Spotsylvania first, barely winning the race on May 8. Confederate cavalry troops held off the advancing Federals west of Spotsylvania (at the battlefield's Laurel Hill site) while the rest of Lee's army prepared defensive positions to the northeast. By the morning of May 9, the Confederates were firmly dug in, with an extensive series of trenches curving for over a mile north of Brock Road between Laurel Hill and Spotsylvania Court House.

This compass, signifying the directions and distances of several nearby towns, bears silent witness to the Wilderness area's importance as a major crossroads for the armies of the North and South.

Lee's soldiers desperately raced across these rolling fields in their determination to beat Grant's Yankees to Spotsylvania.

157

*The serenity of this scene at the Bloody Angle belies the savage combat waged here in the spring of 1864. On these fields, thousands died.*

Grant posted the Army of the Potomac in a 4-mile arc north of the rebel earthworks, probing the western end of the Confederate defenses with two ineffectual assaults on May 10. He then directed Col. Emory Upton to attack the center of Lee's forces, where the Southerners' earthworks bulged forward for half a mile in an inverted U (earning the area its present-day designation as the Mule Shoe salient). Upton's attack was not properly supported and the Yankees eventually had to retreat, but their initial success convinced Grant that the Confederate center was vulnerable.

At dawn on May 12 the Union army launched a full-scale assault against the Mule Shoe salient. Hancock's troops led the charge, fighting like madmen and rushing forward a half mile to McCoull House (a major landmark of today's battlefield park). The Confederates, urged on by General Lee, soon rallied and pushed the Yankees back to the northern end of the Mule Shoe, where Hancock's soldiers were reinforced. Then it was the Northerners turn to rally. They stopped the rebel counterattack in fierce hand-to-hand combat, battling the Southerners for 18 hours at a point on the Mule Shoe aptly dubbed Spotsylvania's "Bloody Angle." Finally, after fighting furiously all day, the Confederates relinquished their hold on the Mule Shoe and retreated to a new line of defense which had been prepared near Brock Road (known today as Lee's Final Line site).

Grant attempted to penetrate Lee's new position several times between May 12 and 18 but without success. On May 19, with the Union offensive at Spotsylvania Court House stalled, Grant again marched the Army of the Potomac to the south to get around Lee's flank. Although the Yankees had lost another 18,000 men at Spotsylvania, the Union commander was determined to continue drawing the rebels into combat along the route to Richmond. Grant knew that Lee's army had suffered equally heavy casualties in the recent fighting and that while the North could replace its losses, the South could not. He planned to keep chipping away at the Army of Northern Virginia in a bloody war of attrition until the rebels could simply no longer fight.

PETERSBURG

Lt. Gen. Ulysses S. Grant continued moving the Army of the Potomac south after the Battle of Spotsylvania, attempting to outflank Gen. Robert E. Lee's Army of Northern Virginia. By late May the two armies had fought their way to the very outskirts of Richmond, with Lee's troops still interposed between the Yankees and the Confederate capital. On June 3, 1864, the Union commander tried fighting his way through the Confederate defenses east of Richmond at Cold Harbor, Virginia, but was repulsed with heavy losses.

With the Federal campaign against Richmond checked, Grant decided to resume his army's march southward to Petersburg, Virginia, a vital railroad hub 20 miles beyond Richmond.

Petersburg's five rail lines served as the Southern army's main source of supplies; if the Yankees could seize the town, they could starve Lee's troops into submission. In addition, by moving against Petersburg, they would compel the rebels to divide their already weakened forces between the defense of the railhead and the Confederate capital.

The Army of the Potomac left Cold Harbor on June 12 and proceeded to cross the James River toward Petersburg, which lay on the south side of the Appomattox River 9 miles west of its junction with the James. Maj. Gen. William F. Smith's 15,000 Yankees were the first Federal troops to arrive, approaching the outer line of rebel defenses northeast of the city on June 15. The Confederate fortifications consisted of a series of earthworks set on a high ridge which looked impossible

*General Grant's headquarters on the grounds of Appomattox Manor at City Point, 7 miles northeast of the siege lines that surrounded Petersburg. Grant kept informed of battlefield developments via field telegraph.*

to assault. In fact, the works were garrisoned by fewer than 2500 soldiers and Smith's Northerners could have easily stormed them, but it took the Union general most of the day to determine this. Smith finally launched an assault late in the afternoon, and by nightfall his troops captured several Confederate positions (including the Petersburg Battlefield Park's Batteries 8 and 9).

The Union soldiers held off further attacks against Petersburg until the rest of the Army of the Potomac's 90,000 troops arrived. On June 17, the Federal offensive resumed with Grant's capture of Hare House Hill southwest of Batteries 8 and 9.

The two-day delay in Federal offensives (between June 15 and 17) destroyed Grant's chance of seizing the city quickly. Indeed, by the evening of June 17, Lee had sent 50,000 soldiers from Richmond, making Petersburg's defenses truly formidible. The Army of the Potomac attempted to storm the rebel lines on June 18 but was turned back with heavy losses. Realizing that his troops could not take the town by direct assault, Grant reluctantly ordered a siege as a means of keeping Lee bottled up until the Army of Northern Virginia surrendered. To achieve Grant's objective, the Yankees commenced constructing a series of trenches and earthworks opposite the rebel defenses, continually extending their lines to the south and west in an effort to encircle the city. Among the first of these fortifications was Fort Steadman, erected atop Hare House Hill (a major stop on today's battlefield tour).

As the siege wore on with no sign of ending, one of Grant's units composed of Pennsylvania coal miners proposed a way to speed up the Northern offensive. They offered to dig a

*The site of Battery Nine, which was captured by African-American soldiers under the command of Brig. Gen. Edward Hinks on the first day of the Union campaign against Petersburg.*

tunnel under the Confederate lines about a mile south of Fort Stedman and blow an opening in the rebel breastworks with black powder. Grant approved, and by July 23 the miners had tunneled 585 feet to—and 20 feet below—the Confederate's Fort Elliott.

At 4:45 a.m. on July 30, the miners exploded 4 tons of gunpowder beneath the rebel fort, opening a gap 30 feet deep and 80 feet across the Southern defenses—the battlefield's famous "Crater." Thousands of Union troops, part of the hapless Maj. Gen. Ambrose E. Burnside's command, poured into the Crater only to discover that they could not climb out of the hole and were trapped there. The Confederates, temporarily stunned by the tremendous explosion, quickly recovered their wits and massed around the rim of the Crater, pouring a deadly fire into the helpless Yankees below. Before the Federal troops were finally withdrawn at 1 p.m., they had suffered more than 4400 casualties in this most unusual assault of the war.

After the costly debacle at the Crater, Grant returned to his strategy of extending the Union siege lines around Petersburg. By mid-August, the Army of the Potomac's earthworks stretched for 6 miles beyond Fort Stedman to Fort Wadsworth, a battlefield site due south of Petersburg, and Grant's soldiers had cut off three of the city's railroad lines. When Federal operations ceased for the winter in October, the line had been extended 2 more miles west to Forts Urmston and Conahey. Like most of the forts outside Petersburg, these were named for Union commanders who had been killed during the army's campaign from the Wilderness to Petersburg.

Although the Federal offensive against Petersburg slowed down in October, Lee's besieged army received little relief. Grant had succeeded in cutting off most of the Confederates' food supplies, and the soldiers in Petersburg, ill-fed and poorly clothed, suffered from exposure throughout the

(Opposite page) *The foundations of the Taylor Farm, near the spot where Union miners began their tunnel under the rebel lines. Almost 200 artillery pieces were massed here to provide covering fire during the assault on the Crater.*

A Federal infantry regiment. During the siege of Petersburg, U.S. troops were as well uniformed and equipped as these soldiers, but Lee's Confederates had almost no access to new arms or clothing.

*One of the roadways of the Petersburg National Battlefield Park.*

The grave of an unknown soldier at the Poplar Grove National Cemetery, south of Petersburg. More than 4000 unidentified casualties are buried here.

The Artillery Monument in the Poplar Grove National Cemetery.

*This monument commemorates the battle at Five Forks, where Maj. Gen. Philip H. Sheridan's cavalry troopers cut off Lee's final route of escape south of Petersburg.*

winter. The Union commander kept up the pressure with an attack on February 5, 1865, which secured a Federal base on the western approach to Petersburg near Fort Gregg (also on the battlefield tour). By the spring, the Army of Northern Virginia was near starvation and almost surrounded.

Lee reacted to his predicament with typical daring: he would put his troops on the offensive, attacking the Federals where they least expected it. Early on the morning of March 25, Confederate troops stole into Fort Stedman under cover of darkness and quietly subdued its garrison, fanning out behind Stedman to attack other fortifications they mistakenly thought were in the area. By the time they discovered their error and returned to Stedman, their assault had been discovered and they were forced back to their own lines by heavy fire from neighboring Fort Haskell (a battlefield site south of Stedman). The fruitless attack had cost Lee more than 4000 soldiers.

Following this audacious rebel raid, Grant became worried that Lee would somehow escape from Petersburg. Consequently, he renewed his efforts to secure the city, extending the Federal trenches another mile farther west to Fort Fisher and stretching Lee's undermanned defenses to the breaking point. Grant also sent cavalry troops under Maj. Gen. Philip H. Sheridan to capture the village of Five Forks, 12 miles to the southwest, thus cutting off Lee's last supply line and escape route to the south.

On April 2, Lee, recognizing the hopelessness of his situation, advised Confederate President Davis that his troops would have to abandon both Petersburg and Richmond. He began pulling his army out of the former that night, crossing the Appomattox River northward to join with Lt. Gen. James C. Longstreet's command from Richmond. The Yankees attempted to stop the Confederate evacuation but were held back in a last-ditch defense by 600 southerners at Fort Gregg. This stand bought Lee the time he needed to leave the city. By dawn on April 3, 1865, Federal troops had occupied both Petersburg and Richmond, and the war was nearing its end.

*The first Federal wagon train to enter the
surrendered city of Petersburg. (Library of
Congress)*

APPOMATTOX

*Maj. Gen. Philip H. Sheridan, whose cavalry troopers finally trapped the fleeing Confederate army at Appomattox Court House. (Library of Congress)*

*The Clover Hill Tavern, built in 1819, is the oldest building standing at Appomattox Court House.*

*(Previous page) These headstones mark the final resting place of a group of Confederate soldiers who, exhausted and ill, could travel no farther.*

When Gen. Robert E. Lee removed his troops from Richmond and Petersburg, Virginia, he knew that they could not possibly defeat Lt. Gen. Ulysses S. Grant's Army of the Potomac unaided. His only dim hope lay in joining with Gen. Joseph E. Johnston's army, then in North Carolina. If their combined forces could defeat Maj. Gen. William T. Sherman's Yankees in the Carolinas, the Confederacy might still have a chance for independence.

Lee planned to have his divided forces meet at Amelia Court House, 35 miles west of Petersburg. (Like other "Court Houses" in Virginia, the town's name signifies that it is the county seat.) From there, the army could travel into North Carolina on the Richmond & Danville Railroad. The scattered remnants of Lee's command began assembling at Amelia Court House on April 4, 1865. Among the early arrivals was Lee himself, traveling with Longstreet's forces. Behind them were the commands of Brig. Gen. John B. Gordon and Lt. Gen. Richard H. Anderson from Petersburg, followed on April 3 by the troops of Lt. Gen. Richard S. Ewell and Maj. Gen. William Mahone from Richmond. The once proud Army of Northern Virginia now numbered only 30,000 ragged, hungry men.

As Lee marched westward, Federal cavalry troops under Maj. Gen. Philip H. Sheridan set out to cut off the rebels' paths of escape. On April 4, Sheridan arrived at Jetersville, 10 miles south of Amelia Court House, where he discovered that the Richmond & Danville Railroad was no longer operating. With Lee's southerly rail route closed, Sheridan proceeded to block the roadway in order to prevent the Confederates from marching to North Carolina.

When Lee found that the railroad was not in service on April 5, he started his army down the road to Jetersville as Sheridan had anticipated. Discovering his path blocked, Lee decided to march his troops *around* the Federal lines rather than risk a fight. The exhausted rebels continued

*The approach to Appomattox Court House, Virginia. The entire village has been restored to its 1865 appearance by the National Park Service.*

*The Isbell House, which stands south of the Surrender Triangle, was owned in 1865 by Virginia's Commonwealth Attorney, Lewis D. Isbell.*

*From the porch of the Kelly House, shown here, local residents may well have watched the soldiers of the Army of Northern Virginia stack their arms for the last time in April 1865.*

*The only Union soldier buried at Appomattox Court House (left) and Alabama's J. H. Hutchins (above) serve as solitary reminders of the war's devastating cost to both North and South.*

*The Mariah Wright House, where Union troops camped before the surrender.*

their trek westward, unaware that Sheridan's cavalry was already racing ahead to cut them off. Meanwhile, the Army of the Potomac was rapidly closing in from behind.

The advancing Federals caught up with the fleeing and starving Southerners on April 6 at Saylor's Creek, a stream 7 miles west of Jetersville. The commands of Longstreet and Mahone made it safely across the creek before the Yankees arrived and most of Gordon's units escaped northward, but Anderson and Ewell's troops were trapped between Sheridan's cavalry and Maj. Gen. Horatio G. Wright's infantry. After a heated fight at the Battle of Saylor's Creek, which marked the final combat of the Army of Northern Virginia, most of Anderson and Ewell's soldiers were captured. On hearing

that his hard-pressed forces had thus lost 8000 men, Lee could only exclaim in despair, "My God, has this army dissolved?"

Following the Confederate losses at Saylor's Creek, Grant felt that Lee might be willing to surrender, and on April 7 sent him a request to discuss terms. Lee was not yet ready to give up, though, and continued his army's march to the west, futilely trying to outrun the pursuing Army of the Potomac. On the evening of April 8, the last remnants of the Army of Northern Virginia arrived near Appomattox Court House to find their route west cut off by Sheridan's cavalry. By the next morning the Federal infantry had moved up behind them, and the Southerners were trapped.

Lee, realizing that his situation was hopeless and anxious to avoid needless bloodshed, sent word to Grant

that he wished to discuss terms. Grant agreed to such a discussion and aides were dispatched to Appomattox Court House to find a suitable meeting place. They selected the home of Wilmer McLean, which has been reconstructed as a focal point of the Appomattox Court House National Historical Park. McLean had previously lived in Manassas, Virginia, but after the two battles there he moved to Appomattox to avoid the warring armies. In one of the strangest coincidences in American history, the Civil War had found McLean one more time.

The South's last hurrah: A reenactment formation similar to that of Lee's Army of Northern Virginia at Appomattox. There, at the Surrender Triangle, many Confederate units tore their colors (like the flag at left) to pieces, dividing the cloth among the men, rather than surrendering their beloved battle flags to the Yankees. The soldiers laid down their rifles, bayonets, and cartridge boxes (the leather pouches on their right hips) and went home.

Lee and his aides arrived at the McLean house in the early afternoon, followed by Grant and his staff about a half hour later. After exchanging pleasantries in the parlor for a few minutes, Lee asked Grant for his terms of surrender. The Union commander demanded that Lee's soldiers relinquish their arms and supplies and agree to not fight any further; in return, they would be released to go home. Grant also permitted all officers to keep their horses and sidearms, the latter freeing them from the embarrassment of surrendering their swords. At Lee's request he also allowed the rebel cavalry troopers to keep their horses and mules, as the animals would be needed for spring planting. The Confederate com-

mander quickly agreed to these terms, and the surrender papers were drawn up and signed. The war had ended for the Army of Northern Virginia.

Lee returned to his headquarters (the site of which has been preserved at the northeast corner of Appomattox historical park) to bid farewell to his troops, and Grant issued instructions to distribute rations to the famished Southerners. The Union commander also banned any victory celebrations by the Federal army, impressing upon his men that the Confederates were no longer foes but fellow countrymen. Reflecting President Lincoln's sentiments, Grant wanted the long road to reconciliation to start at Appomattox "with malice toward none; with charity for all."

On the morning of April 12, 1865, the last 28,231 soldiers of the Army of Northern Virginia surrendered their

arms at a three-sided field behind the court house building—Appomattox's "surrender triangle." As they marched there down the Old Richmond Stage Road, they were saluted by onlooking Union troops in a final show of respect. The Confederates returned the compliment, laid down their weapons, and left to begin their lives anew. In little more than a month, the last remaining Confederate troops outside of Virginia surrendered and the war was over. After four years of bloody struggle, the country was again united. Abraham Lincoln, tragically assassinated five days after the surrender at Appomattox, had achieved his goal: the government of the people, by the people, for the people, had not perished from the earth.

*Gen. Robert E. Lee, defeated but unbowed, astride his horse Traveller as they appeared at Appomattox. (Eleanor S. Brockenbrough Library, The Museum of the Confederacy, Richmond, Virginia)*

*(Following page) The McLean House, site of Lee's surrender. The original building was dismantled in 1893, and plans to reconstruct it failed to materialize until this replica was erected by the National Park Service in 1949.*